Winning Backgammon

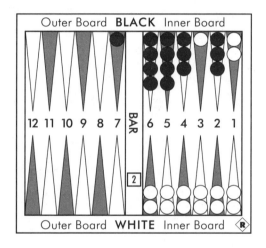

John Leet

STERLING PUBLISHING CO., INC.
New York

Library of Congress Cataloging-in-Publication Data

Leet, John.
    Winning backgammon / John Leet.
        p.   cm.
    Includes index.
    ISBN 0-8069-0459-3
    1. Backgammon.   I. Title.
GV1469.B2L44 1998
795.1'5–dc21   97-46176
                             CIP

10 9 8 7 6 5 4 3 2 1

Published by Sterling Publishing Company, Inc.
387 Park Avenue South, New York, N.Y. 10016
© 1998 by John Leet
Distributed in Canada by Sterling Publishing
%Canadian Manda Group, One Atlantic Avenue, Suite 105
Toronto, Ontario, Canada M6K 3E7
Distributed in Great Britain and Europe by Cassell PLC
Wellington House, 125 Strand, London WC2R 0BB, England
Distributed in Australia by Capricorn Link (Australia) Pty Ltd.
P.O. Box 6651, Baulkham Hills, Business Centre, NSW 2153, Australia

Sterling ISBN 0-8069-0459-3

CONTENTS

FOREWORD

This is a refreshing, concise, easy-to-understand guide for one of the world's oldest games, backgammon. The objective of this book is to rejuvenate interest in and expand the popularity of this intriguing game. Unfortunately, backgammon has been misunderstood and underrated in the past, and many people have needlessly lost interest in the game. An enhanced framework for playing the game is presented here to make it much better understood and more rewarding.

When the real game of backgammon is understood and properly played, skill dominates and luck is only a small but important factor. Complete coverage and explanation of the winning strategy is provided without getting bogged down in mathematical details. More than 120 strategy principles are explained, and nearly 100 figures and tables are included to illustrate the correct strategy. This will make you a winner and will make this excellent game enjoyable.

1. A Uniquely Fascinating Game

I have found backgammon to be an intriguing, fascinating, and challenging game. One can quickly learn the game's mechanics and may come to the conclusion that luck dominates so that the person who gets the higher dice rolls will invariably win. The impression is gotten that the game is merely a race around the board where the luckiest player wins. Actually, the game has an enormous amount of strategy, and a player who applies the correct strategy will beat someone who doesn't a high percentage of the time. In fact, when the game is played properly, a player who uses the correct strategy will beat an average player 85% to 95% of the time. If you learn and apply the strategy that I provide and explain in this book, *you* will win a high percentage of the time (unless you're playing someone else who has read and taken this book to heart).

Most people who play backgammon have not learned how to play the game properly and have not learned the correct strategy. As a result, they tried backgammon and found it to be boring and dominated by luck. They soon lost interest and stopped playing it. Those that realized that there is considerable strategy involved saw the strategy as being tedious to learn and also lost interest. This is unfortunate, because when played properly backgammon is a fascinating (even exciting) and challenging game. While there are many mathematical details needed for the fine points of the game, most of the correct strategy that makes a winner can be easily learned.

Admittedly, bridge and chess are more popular games. But backgammon has several aspects that make it a better game. For many, both bridge and chess are too dry, involved, and slow-moving, and they demand a high degree of intense, prolonged concentration. On the other hand, backgammon is much, much easier to learn, it is fast-moving and lighthearted, and it is exciting because the lead can change hands quickly. It is a dynamic game where the situation is constantly changing—there is always the possibility of large changes in fortune. No two games are the same, and there are no anticlimactic draws in backgammon. All that is needed to have a rewarding game are two people who know how to play the game properly and a backgammon set. A set is less expensive than an electronic or computer game and provides much more enduring enjoyment. If you have a computer with a good backgammon game (a number of them are available), you don't even need another person. You can even play on the Internet. However, you're in backgammon heaven if three or more other players are available to have a mini-tournament.

In this book I will describe the proper way to play backgammon in a manner that is easy to understand. As you will see, the way to play backgammon is with the doubling cube and to play one or more sets, rather than isolated games. The mistakes that most people have made in the past are to play without the doubling cube, to play isolated games, and not to learn much of the real strategy. The doubling cube doesn't have much significance unless you play sets and matches or play for money. With the doubling cube, you play for points rather than games per se. In most games the winning player wins one to four points. In some games more than four points are won depending on the doubling cube, gammons, and backgammons.

Tennis has the right idea in that it's played in points, games, sets, matches, and tournaments. The best way to play backgammon is similar to tennis: It should be played in games, points, sets, matches, and tournaments. A player wins one or more points by winning a game, and wins a set by winning a predetermined number of points. The recommended set size is seven points. The first player who wins seven (or more) points wins the set. This allows a match to consist of several sets, increases strategy, and reduces the element of luck and impact of an unfortunate game. In a tournament, the player who wins the match advances to the next round, and the player who wins every round is the tournament champion. However, two players (or a player and a computer) can have a rewarding backgammon session by playing a match that consists of one seven-point set.

Backgammon can also be rewarding if played for money, where a point, set, match, and tournament are each worth a predetermined amount of money. Whether played for money, glory, or love of the game, all of the elements and strategy of backgammon come into play and are important, including the doubling cube and roll-over. If the game is played for a given amount of money for each point, most, but not all, of the strategy comes into play.

I highly recommend that the roll-over variant be used (see page 18 and Chapter 5) because it adds strategy and reduces the element of luck. It adds another dimension to the game. The roll-over should be limited to one use for each player each game. While the roll-over reduces the amount of luck somewhat, there is still enough left in the game to make it exciting.

You will need to read the rest of this book to learn the rules, mechanics, and strategy of backgammon, but the preceding paragraphs provide an overview of the proper framework for playing the game. When backgammon is played in this framework with the correct strategy, it can be an intriguing and gratifying game in which luck plays a reasonably small role. Luck is a large enough element to make the game interesting, exciting, and addictive, but it isn't a large factor; not nearly as large as many people think. When two evenly matched players are playing each other, luck plays a larger role, as it does in just about any game or sport. One of the keys to playing backgammon well, as in most games, is to minimize the impact of bad luck and take maximum advantage of good luck. The game is far from a mere race around the board where the player who gets the higher dice rolls wins. Actually, high dice rolls are often disastrous.

Backgammon has a long fascinating history of more than 5000 years, making it one of the oldest games in civilization. The earliest backgammon board, from an early version of the game, was found circa 3000 B.C. in the royal cemetery in Ur of the Chaldees in southern Mesopotamia (now Iraq), the birthplace of Abraham.

The game has been played around the world and throughout recorded history. A form of the game was enjoyed by the Egyptian Pharaohs; boards dating from 1500 B.C. were found in King Tut's tomb. Wall paintings in many Egyptian tombs portray people playing the game, indicating that it was played by the common people as well as the Pharaohs. A thousand years later the Greeks were playing a form of the game. Homer, Sophocles, and Plato mention the game in their works. In Rome, the game long remained one of the most popular among the patricians. Emperor Claudius reportedly wrote a book on backgammon. The excavators of Pompeii found a backgammon table in the courtyard of almost every villa. Various early versions of the game were popular in Britain, dating from the Crusades. It has always been a favorite game of the English. It is believed that the current form of the game evolved in the tenth century. Backgammon has been played in the United States since the seventeenth century. Edmond Hoyle systematized and documented the rules in 1743.

The doubling cube was introduced to the game (in the United States) in the early 1920s by an anonymous genius. This greatly enhanced the quality of backgammon and increased its popularity in this country. The game had another surge of interest in the 1970s, but has waned in popularity in recent years due primarily to the advent of video and computer games.

Hopefully, interest in this ancient game will increase in the future. Perhaps if more people discover the real game of backgammon, as presented in this book, it will regain the popularity that it deserves.

I sincerely hope that this book will stimulate your interest in backgammon, and improve your ability to play the game so that you will win the vast majority of your matches. If this happens, my objective will have been accomplished.

2. Rules and Mechanics of the Game

Backgammon rules are provided in Appendix A. They are short, simple, and easy to remember. Take a couple minutes now to read them if you aren't already familiar with them. Although it's possible to learn the mechanics of the game by reading the rules, I will explain them in this chapter. It's important that you have a solid and fluent understanding of the mechanics that comply with the rules. I will provide and explain the game's strategy in the remaining chapters. Get your backgammon set out, arrange it to match the situations, and perform the moves as you read this book. Then find someone to play some sets and matches to start enjoying the fun and excitement of this intriguing game. After you whup him a few times, introduce him to this book.

GAME SETUP

The setup at the beginning of each game is shown in Figure 2-1. The following things are needed to play and are contained in a backgammon set.

- A board, divided by the bar into inner (home) and outer boards as shown in Figure 2-1.
- 30 men, 15 each of two different colors.
- Two pairs of dice and two dice cups, one for each player.
- A doubling cube.

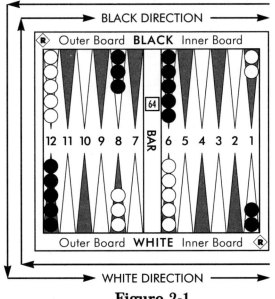

Figure 2-1

• Two roll-over markers, one for each player, indicated by the diamonds containing the letter R in Figure 2-1. Roll-over markers are usually not included in backgammon sets, but anything the size of a coin will work.

It's customary to have the inner boards nearer to the light. Figure 2-1 shows:

• The beginning positions of the men.
• The direction each color moves around the board.
• The doubling cube with 64 on top to indicate the initial basic game value of 1 point since the lowest number on the cube is 2 rather than 1.
• Six triangles in each board, called points, which are numbered 1 to 12 from the inner to outer boards. The 7-points are also called bar points. (The point numbers don't actually appear on backgammon boards.)
• The bar where men are placed when they are hit.
• The runners are the two men on the 1-point for each color. They have the longest distance to travel to get borne off.

In this book, you'll be seated at the bottom of the board playing the white men, and your opponent will play the black men. Each player sits on the side that has his inner and outer boards.

OBJECT OF THE GAME

The object of the game is to move all of your men around into your inner board, then bear them all off from the board. The first player to bear all of his men off wins the game, winning one or more points. A game can have a value of two or more points due to doubling, a gammon, or a backgammon. This will be explained later in this chapter.

A player wins a set by winning a predetermined number of points. In the recommended set size, the first player who wins seven (or more) points wins. A player doesn't have to be two points ahead to win a set; that is, a player can win a set with a score of seven to six. A player can win a set by winning just one game if the game is worth seven or more points.

A match consists of one or more sets. In a three-set match, the player who wins two sets wins the match. In a five-set match, the player who wins three sets wins the match. It's better to have more short sets in a match than one long set. This reduces the element of luck by minimizing the impact of an unfortunate game. Players can keep track of the score with pencil and paper or by using chips to indicate the number of points and sets that each player has won.

BEGINNING A GAME

To start a game each player rolls one of his dice. The player that rolls the higher number moves first using the numbers on the top of both dice (his own and the opponent's) that were rolled. If the players roll the same number, they roll again until they roll different numbers. After the first player completes his move, the other player rolls both of his dice to move. The players then alternate turns, rolling both of their dice and moving their men for the remainder of the game. A round consists of one turn by each player.

Players should put their dice in a dice cup, shake them, and roll the dice from the cup. If acceptable to both players, the players' hands can be used instead of the dice cups to make rolling faster and quieter. The dice pair must be rolled together and both must come to rest completely flat on the board to the player's right; not on any of the men, the bar, the left board, or off the board. Otherwise, the dice are cocked and both must be rolled again.

Most players today modify Rule 16 (see Appendix A) so that a player signifies that his move is completed by picking up his dice. Then the move cannot be changed if it is legal. The move *can* be changed prior to picking up the dice. However, get into the habit of making deliberate moves without changing them. If a lot of changes are made during a turn, it becomes difficult for the players to keep track of where the men were at the beginning of the turn. If this becomes the case, insist on strict adherence to Rule 16. Players should move their men with only one hand to avoid confusion.

MOVES

Each player's turn consists of rolling his dice and moving one to four of his men. The number on each die is played separately, in either order, by moving either one or two men. For example, a 6-4 (6 and 4) roll is played in one of the following ways:
• Move a man 6 points, then another man 4 points.
• Move a man 4 points, then another man 6 points.
• Move one man 6 points and then 4 points.
• Move one man 4 points and then 6 points.

It shouldn't be counted as a 10. If a player rolls doubles (also called doublets), both dice are the same number and that number can and must be played four times instead of two times. For example, a 5-5 roll is played by moving one, two, three, or four men in any combination for a total of four moves of 5 points each. One of the possible combinations is to move one man all four moves, and another possible combination is to move four men 5 points each.

A player cannot move to or touch down on a point that the opponent has made (owns) by having two or more of his men on the point. A man can pass over points owned by the opponent and those points are counted in the move. Both colors of men cannot occupy a point at the same time, but there can be an unlimited number of men of the same color on a point. If a player has only one man on a point, he has not made that point; the man is called a blot, and it can be hit. If a player moves to or touches down on a point that has only one of the opponent's men, that blot is hit and put on the bar to be entered. A man is always safe unless it is the only man on a point.

If black rolls a 4-3 in Figure 2-2, the man (blot) on white's 10-point cannot be moved 3 points, then 4 points because white owns black's 12 point. The man can, however, be moved 4 points, then 3 points to safety on black's 8-point. Another way that black can play the 4-3 roll is to move from white's 1-point to white's 5-point hitting white's blot, then move another man that can move 3 points.

If instead it is white's turn and white rolls a 5-3 in Figure 2-2, a man on black's 12-point can be moved 3 points hitting

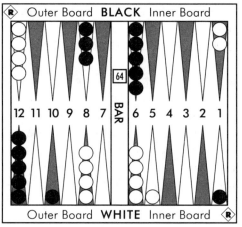

Figure 2-2

black's blot, then moved 5 points to make white's 5-point. White can avoid hitting the blot, if desired, by moving the man (from the 12-point) 5 points first, then 3 points to make the 5-point.

If black rolls 3-3 in Figure 2-2, the blot on the 10-point cannot be moved because it cannot be moved 3 points. This is the only man that black cannot move. A decent move is to use three of the moves to move the runner on the 1-point to cover the blot on the 10-point (making the 10-point), then use the fourth move by moving a man from the 12-point to black's 10-point.

A player must play all of his roll, if possible. If a player can only play one of the numbers rolled, he must play the higher number, if possible.

The points have two alternating colors to help you quickly count the points for your moves. Also, each board has six points so a roll of 6 will move a man from a point in one board to the same point in the next board. The bar isn't counted as a point.

ENTERING FROM THE BAR

When a man (blot) is hit, it is placed on the bar regardless of where it was. If a player has one or more men on the bar, he must enter all of them first before he can make any other move. Men are entered from the bar onto a point in the opponent's inner board according to the number rolled on a die. For example, a 4-2 roll can enter a white man onto black's 4-point or 2-point. A man cannot be entered onto a point that the opponent owns. If all of the men on the bar cannot be entered, then the player cannot move any other man during that turn.

If a player has one man on the bar and rolls a 6-5, the man on the bar must be entered first using the 6 or 5. In this example, assume the opponent still owns his 6-point. If the opponent also owns his 5-point, no move can be made. If the opponent does not own his 5-point, the 5 must be used to enter the man onto the opponent's 5-point. The 6 can then be used to move the entered man to the 11-point or to move any other man that can move 6 points.

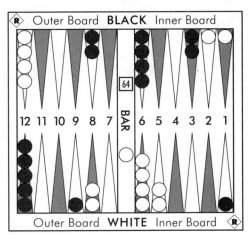

Figure 2-3

In Figure 2-3, white has rolled a 4-3. The man on the bar must first be entered onto black's 4-point using the 4 since black owns his 3-point. Then that man, or any other man that can be moved 3 points, can be moved 3 points. Black's blots cannot be hit this turn since white has to use the 4 to enter.

BEARING OFF

As soon as a player has moved all of his men into his inner board, he can start bearing off (removing men from the board). Once a man is borne off, it doesn't return to play (until the next game). A player cannot start bearing off until all of his men are in his inner board. After a player has started bearing off, he can continue bearing off only if all of his remaining men are in his inner board. If a player's man is hit while he is bearing off, he cannot continue bearing off until the man that was hit has entered and returned to the player's inner board. A player doesn't need to have all of his men in his inner board to advance men within his inner board. Also, a player doesn't have to bear a man off if the roll can be played legally otherwise. Bearing off can be treacherous when your opponent has men in your inner board or on the bar.

When bearing off, a player bears a man off from the point whose number corresponds to a number rolled. A man on the highest point occupied can and must be borne off if the number rolled is equal to or higher than that point. If a player has an unoccupied point with one or more men on a higher point in his inner board, no man can be borne off for a number rolled that is the same as the unoccupied point.

For example, a 5-3 roll bears a man off from the 5-point and a man off from the 3-point. If there are no men on the 5-point or 6-point, the 5 bears a man off from the highest occupied point. If there are no men on the 3-point with one or more men on higher points, the 3 must be used to advance a man within the inner board from a higher point.

In Figure 2-4, black has rolled a 6-4. Black must bear a man off from his 6-point with the 6. A man could be borne off from the 4-point with the 4, but that would leave a blot. It's better for black to move a man from his 6-point to his 2-point with the 4.

In Figure 2-5, white has rolled a 6-3. White can and must bear a man off from his 5-point with the 6. A man can-

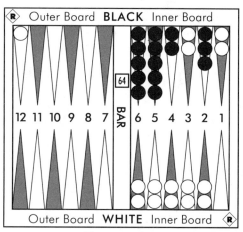

Figure 2-4

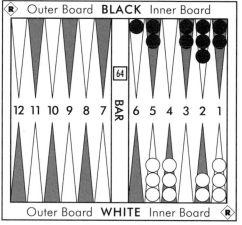

Figure 2-5

not be borne off with the 3 since the 3-point is empty. The 3 has to be used to either move a man from the 5-point to the 2-point or from the 4-point to the 1-point.

GAMMON AND BACKGAMMON

A gammon (double game) is won if the opponent hasn't borne off a single man when the winner bears his last man off. This doubles the game value. A backgammon (triple game) is won if the opponent hasn't borne off a single man and has one or more men in the winner's inner board or on the bar. This triples the game value. A gammon or backgammon can make the game costly for a player who is playing a back game or who doesn't use the correct strategy.

DOUBLING

When a player thinks he has a sufficient lead in a game, he can offer to double the game value to win more points (or money) by winning the game. Either player may offer the first double of the game value by turning the doubling cube to put the 2 on top. After that, the right to double the previous value alternates, being always with the player who has accepted the last double. A double may be offered only when it's the player's turn to play and before he has rolled the dice. A double is either accepted or declined. If the double is accepted, the accepting player puts the cube (with the new game value on top) on his end of the bar and the game continues. The accepting player owns the cube and is the only player who can offer the next double. If the double is declined, the doubled player resigns, the game is terminated, and the doubling player wins the game value at that time (prior to the declined double). Gammons and backgammons double or triple the final game value.

For example, if the first double of a game is declined, the doubling player wins 1 point. If only one double is accepted, the cube has 2 on top and the winner of the game wins 2 points. If the last accepted double puts the cube at 4, the winner of the game wins 4 points. If the cube is at 2 and a backgammon is won, the winner of the game wins 6 points (2 × 3 points).

The doubling rule adds a tremendous amount of strategy to backgammon if the game is played in sets and matches or for money. It also adds excitement and prevents many uninteresting games from being continued when one player has a large lead because that player will double the other player out.

CRAWFORD RULE

When a player gets to one point short of winning a set, the doubling cube cannot be used in the next game, but can be used again thereafter in the set. This rule is usually used in tournaments. It should be used all of the time because it gives the leading player a fairer chance of winning the set by delaying the trailing player's ability to double abnormally to catch up. This provides a game in most sets that is completed by bearing off all of the winner's men (neither player is doubled out).

In a seven-point set, doubling is not allowed if and when the leading player first has six points. If the leading player doesn't win that game (to win the set), then doubling is allowed again for the rest of the set. The Crawford Rule doesn't come into play in a set where the set winner wins two or more points in the final game, skipping over being one point short of the set.

ROLL-OVER

Once during each game, each player can decide either to roll again or to have his opponent roll again. A player must decide to roll again before he picks up his dice; that is, before he completes his turn. A player can wait until his opponent completes his turn (seeing how he moves) before deciding to have the opponent roll again; however, the player must decide before rolling for his turn. The opponent cannot double before rolling again; he must wait until the next turn to double. Each player starts each game with a roll-over marker and removes it from the board when he exercises his roll-over option.

The roll-over is actually a variant that was introduced to backgammon by Richard Frey in the 1960s. I highly recommend that this variant be used because it adds strategy, reduces the element of luck, and reduces frustration. It provides additional interest and excitement to the game. The roll-over should be limited to one for each player each game, and must be agreed upon by all players or the tournament director before it is adopted in a session or tournament.

OPTIONAL RULES

Rules 20a and 21 (see Appendix A) apply only if all players agree to use them. Most players and tournaments don't use them. They should never be used because they aren't compatible with playing backgammon in sets and matches. The game loses much of its quality if it isn't played in sets and matches. The use of these optional rules combined with playing backgammon in isolated games is probably the largest reason (other than the advent of electronic games) that people have lost interest in the game.

VARIANTS

Backgammon variants are described in Chapter 12. Become familiar with them, but the roll-over is the only variant that should be used.

3. Basic Strategy

Now that you have learned the rules and mechanics of backgammon, you're ready for the fun part: learning the strategy and playing the game. First, I will present and explain the basic strategy for winning. Hopefully you still have your backgammon set out, and you will set up the situations and perform the moves as they are described. Throughout the remainder of the book, I will present the main strategy principles in italics, followed by an amplification and explanation of each principle. For many of the principles, one or more subprinciples are identified. For most of the principles, a situation or position is shown and explained to illustrate the principle. Although only one (or sometimes two) representative specific position and roll is shown for each principle, the principle is usually applicable for a range of similar positions and rolls.

I will introduce the principles in the chapter (game phase) where they are most appropriate and easiest to understand. However, most of the principles are applicable, and should be used, during all phases of each game, set, and match. The strategy principles are collected in Appendix B for easy reference. Refer to Appendix B often when you play until all of the strategy principles become second nature.

BASIC GAME SAVVY

3-1. Have a comfortable playing environment so you can concentrate on the game

While backgammon doesn't require intense or prolonged concentration, it does require good concentration during the critical periods of most games. Try to be in a comfortable playing environment, whether you are playing in a tournament, club, or casual session. Factors in the playing environment include board size, table height, chairs, lighting, temperature, smoking, noise, and kibitzers.

3-2. Be able to play at a rapid pace, but do not rush

The game is most enjoyable when it is played at a steady rapid pace. A typical game should take seven to eight minutes. Games will be shorter or longer than that depending on whether and when a player is doubled out. A rapid pace allows a few sets to be played in a reasonable amount of time. Pencil and paper, calculators, and computers shouldn't be used to make calculations during a backgammon session or tournament. Calculations should be done mentally and quickly to keep the game moving at a steady rapid pace. Except for informal sessions, players should not refer to books or notes while playing.

You should be able to play at a rapid pace and should expect the same of your opponent. Play with deliberate haste, but don't rush to the point that you make a mistake. You need to become fluent with the mechanics and strategy so that you can play at a rapid pace always using the correct strategy without making mistakes. You need to constantly assess the situation, including while your opponent is moving, so you can make most moves and doubling decisions quickly. Some moves and decisions, though, will require more time for thinking.

3-3. Become equally comfortable playing with either color men and with your inner board to your left or right

You'll have to play from both sides of the board and with both colors of men so you need to be able to play your best regardless of the color of your men and the direction that you move them. Although you are always playing the white men with your inner board to your right in this book (to avoid confusion), mix it up when you are playing so that it doesn't matter which combination you have in a given game, set, match, or tournament.

3-4. Insist on not using any of the variants or optional rules except the roll-over

The backgammon variants are described in Chapter 12. Familiarize yourself with them, because some players may suggest that one or more of the variants be used. Strongly encourage the use of the roll-over, but be reluctant to use any other variant or optional rule. The other variants and the optional rules generally increase the element of luck and aren't compatible with playing backgammon in sets and matches. Tournaments and most players don't use them. The use of any variant or optional rule must be agreed upon by all players prior to start of play.

3-5. Always check that opponent's move is legal; if opponent makes an illegal move that is unfavorable for you, have him correct it

Remember that you don't have to point out and correct an illegal move by your opponent. If the move is to your advantage, don't say anything. But if the illegal move is unfavorable for you, have him correct it. The rules say that your opponent has to correct the move by moving the man legally if possible, if you point it out before you start your turn. If you determine that you have made an unfavorable illegal move after you pick up your dice, you can correct it if you do so before your opponent starts his turn. Be a good sportsman and don't deliberately make an illegal move.

3-6. Do not let your opponent know he made a mistake; that is, do not help him adjust or improve his game

Don't let your expressions tell your opponent that he has made a good or bad roll, move, double, acceptance, resignation, or roll-over. Play with serious deliberation regardless of whether your decisions are easy or difficult.

3-7. Play to minimize impact of bad luck and take maximum advantage of good luck

As in any game, you'll have both good and bad luck when playing backgammon. You need to know the odds and make moves that won't result in disaster if you have subsequent bad luck. Avoid being doubled out, gammoned, or backgammoned. When you get a really bad roll, look for the least damaging way to play it. When you receive good luck due to a good roll or a mistake by your opponent, capitalize on it by getting into a position to double, gammon, or backgammon your opponent. It is said that chance favors the prepared mind.

3-8. Never give up, even if it appears that you are hopelessly behind

A player's fortune can change suddenly in backgammon, particularly when he uses the correct strategy. Never lose your concentration, get reckless, or give up hope. Keep using the correct strategy to the end. Although it doesn't happen often, players can and have come back to win from what appeared to be a hopeless situation. Give yourself a chance to get lucky. The game's not over till it's over. Always use the correct strategy and decline your opponent's double when it's proper to.

Don't get psyched out by your opponent. Always use logic and the correct strategy, rather than emotions, when making your moves and decisions. If you make a mistake, don't let it result in subsequent mistakes. Of course, it's okay if your opponent makes mistakes as a result of his psychological weakness.

PRIME STRATEGIC OBJECTIVE

3-9. A blocking game is substantially better than a running game, about 65%

Many players, if not most, think that a running game, where they use every roll to try to move their runners and men on the 12-point to the inner board, is best. However, a blocking game, where you give top priority to building a blockade, is the best strategy. A blockade, where you own four or more points close together, makes it difficult for your opponent's men to get past because he cannot land on points that you own. A player that plays a blocking game will beat a player that has the same ability and plays a running game about 65% of the games. Playing a blocking game will make you a winner. In most games you'll be able to build a good blockade in time to trap or slow down one or more of the opponent's men long enough to win.

3-10. Your prime strategy is to build a strong blockade as quickly as possible to trap one of the opponent's men; you will usually have nearly 26 rolls, if necessary, to do this before he finishes bearing off (assuming you are not doubled out)

Since a blocking game is decidedly better than a running game, give top priority to building a strong blockade to trap your opponent. This is an extremely important principle and the cornerstone of the winning strategy. Most of the strategy for moves is aimed at accomplishing this objective. Usually you only have to trap one of the opponent's men to win the game. Quickly try to build a blockade of four or more points in the area between your 3-point and 9-point. Even if you cannot build a blockade rapidly, keep working at it because a blockade completed later will usually pay off. Even if your opponent's runners escape, you'll probably hit a man later to trap behind your blockade.

After you build a four-point blockade, where you own four points within a six-point span, continue to improve it to a five-point blockade and then to a prime. When you have a prime, you own six points in a row and are in an extremely powerful position. Since six points is the largest possible move, it's impossible for your opponent's men to get past your prime. The prime will probably first be a side prime in the area between your 3-point and 9-point. Once you have a side prime, caterpillar it into a true prime where you own your 1-point through 6-point, all of the points in your inner board.

You will see later that it usually takes a player around 26 rolls to get all of his men around and bear them all off if none of his men become trapped. While you should build a blockade as quickly as possible, this shows that you actually have a lot of time, if necessary, to build one. So even if you get hit several times and are having trouble building a blockade, don't lose heart and keep working to form a blockade. But you need to avoid being doubled out in the process.

3-11. Only a slight advantage in winning games is needed to have a large advantage in winning matches

Figure 3-1 shows the probability of winning sets and matches as a function of the probability of winning points. Two players that have an equal ability in every aspect of the game have an equal chance, 50%, of winning games, points, sets, and matches. In other words, they will each win half of the time when they play each other many times. As in any game, if they only play two matches there is no guarantee that they will each win one of the matches, due to the laws of probability and the element of luck. As you can see from Figure 3-1, only a slight advantage in winning points, say 55%, results in a large advantage in winning matches, 76% of three-out-of-five-set matches.

You saw earlier that a player who plays a blocking game will beat a player that has the same ability and plays a running game about 65% of the games. This allows the blocking player to win around 68% of the points. Figure 3-1 shows that the

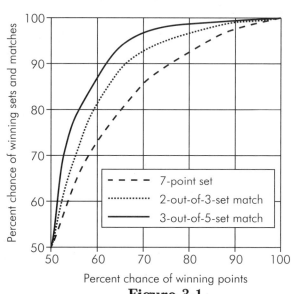

Figure 3-1

blocking player will win about 95% of three-out-of-five-set matches.

A good player that uses all of the correct strategy will beat an average player 60% to 65% of the games. The good player can win 70% of the points (including the effect of doubling, gammons, and backgammons). Figure 3-1 shows that the good player can therefore win 85% of the sets, 92% of two-out-of-three-set matches, and 96% of three-out-of-five-set matches. These high winning percentages show that using the correct strategy is extremely important. Strategy is a large element of backgammon and luck is not a large factor.

Against an inexperienced player, a good player who uses the correct strategy will win an even higher percentage of the time. An expert would win virtually all, 97% to 100%, of the three-out-of-five-set matches against an inexperienced player. If backgammon were dominated by luck and merely a race around the board where the player that gets the higher dice rolls wins, then a player would win only half of the matches regardless of his skill level. The high winning percentages for a good player who uses the correct strategy show that backgammon is far from a game of chance.

FUNDAMENTAL STRATEGY FOR WINNING

3-12. Priority for making points: your 5-, 7-, 4-, 3-, and 9-points, in that order

You saw earlier that your prime strategy is to build a strong blockade to trap your opponent, and that the blockade should be in the area between your 3-point and 9-point. Thus, your top priority is to make points between your 3-point and 9-point. You start each game owning your 6-point and 8-point. To complete a side prime you need to make your 5-, 7-, 4-, and 3- or 9-points, in that order of preference. It is important that you make your 5-point because it is the third point of a four-point blockade, and it is in your inner board, which makes it harder for your opponent to enter men from the bar and puts men in position to allow you to start bearing off later. The 7-point (bar point) is the next most important point to make because it is the fourth point in a four-point blockade. The 4-point is next because it expands your blockade to five points and is in your inner board. The 3-point takes preference to your 9-point in completing your side prime because it is in your inner board, and you'll have less distance to caterpillar the prime. Of course, if you own your 4-point through 8-point, you'll gladly make your 9-point to complete the side prime rather than wait to make your 3-point first.

3-13. You have a greater than 95% chance of winning a game when you trap one or more men behind a prime

It was stated earlier that you are in an extremely powerful position when you form a prime. Once you have one or more of the opponent's men trapped behind your prime, regardless of whether it's a side or true prime, you will virtually always win the game. In this position you have at least a 95% chance of winning the game if you don't have men trapped such that you would have to break your prime before you get them freed. You will almost always be able to caterpillar your prime into a true prime and bear several of your men off before your opponent's man escapes. Then it's much too late for your opponent to win the bearing-off race. Just about the only chance your opponent has is to hit one of your men after you have borne some men off and broken your prime. You aren't likely to have to leave a blot that will be hit. Even if this happens, you're still likely to win.

3-14. Move to form a six-point side prime, then caterpillar it into a true prime

As explained earlier, your primary objective should be to form a blockade in the area between your 3-point and 9-point and improve it into a side prime. Nearly all of your moves should be used toward this objective. Once you have formed a side prime, you need to trap one of the opponent's men behind your prime if a man is not already trapped. Then carefully caterpillar the prime into a true prime always maintaining six points in a row so that it's impossible for your opponent to escape. You do this by making the point in front of the prime with two of your men. Then you can break the point at the back end since it's now the seventh point in a row. You keep repeating this process until your prime is in the six points of your inner board and your opponent's man is on the bar.

Since twelve of your men are needed to form the prime, you must use your other three men to caterpillar it. You can use a man from the back-end point to make the point in front of the prime since this maintains six points in a row. Use double 3s and double 6s to move the men from the back end point to the point in front of the prime to caterpillar it.

If your opponent has two or more men trapped behind your prime and owns one or more points in your inner board, caterpillar your prime to become adjacent to the point that your opponent owns. If your opponent doesn't break the point, then start making points behind your opponent's point and break the point at the back end of your prime when necessary. This will allow your opponent's men to escape, but you still have more than a 90% chance of winning the game and your chance of winning a gammon becomes significant.

3-15. When caterpillaring a prime, move your other men to the prime one at a time to optimize your chance of caterpillaring it

To give yourself the best chance of caterpillaring your prime without having to break a point in it, move your other three men to the front end of your prime one at a time, starting with the closest one. This provides a builder in the prime waiting for a roll to make the point in front of the prime while you move the other men up to the prime. In Figure 3-2, move your man on your 12-point to the front end of your prime before you move the two men that are in your opponent's boards since they are in no danger of being trapped. If you roll a 4-3, move your man from your 12-point to your 5-point. Then a 6-2, 6-6, 3-3, or 2-2 will allow you to make your 3-point to caterpillar the prime. If you don't get one of these rolls, move your man that is on your opponent's 9-point up to the front end of the prime.

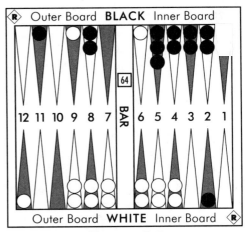

Figure 3-2

3-16. When caterpillaring a prime, put a blot in front of prime when necessary if there is little chance it will be trapped after entering if it is hit

If you roll a 4-2 in Figure 3-3, move a man from your 7-point to the 3-point and a man from your 4-point to the 2-point. Then any 1 or 6 will make your 2-point and caterpillar your prime. If you don't

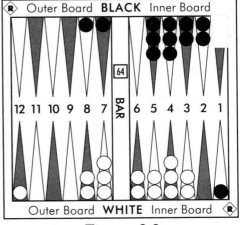

Figure 3-3

28

get a roll that will make the 2-point, move your man from the 12-point. If your blot on the 2-point is hit, it will not be trapped after it enters. If it's hit and cannot enter, you won't have to break your prime because you cannot move any men.

3-17. Achieve as even a distribution as possible

Strive to achieve and maintain an even distribution of your men, which means that you should have two or three men on a point. Sometimes you will have one man (a blot) on a point when trying to make the point. It's good to have a third man on a point to provide a builder to make another point, but it's a waste to have more than three men on a point. While it's important to make points between your 3-point and 9-point to trap your opponent, it's also important to make these points because they provide safe landing spots for your other men.

You have rolled a 5-4 in Figure 3-4. You could move the men on your 10-point and 11-point to the 6-point, but that would produce an uneven distribution. Instead, move the man on the 10-point to the 5-point and the man on the 11-point to the 7-point. This maintains an

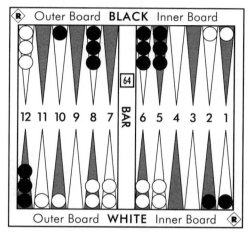

Figure 3-4

even distribution and provides two builders to make your 4-point or 3-point.

3-18. When considerably behind in a game or set, play more aggressively than usual

When you're considerably behind in a game or set, play more aggressively by leaving blots, if necessary, to increase your chance of making points between your 3-point and 9-point and of hitting your opponent. You don't have much to lose and you have a lot to gain by taking more chances to make critical points or hit your opponent. Once you have closed most of the lead, use normal strategy again.

ROLLS REQUIRED TO START AND FINISH BEARING OFF

3-19. Average roll is 8 pips

The average roll is approximately 8 pips (a pip being a move of one point). For example, a 4-3 roll is 7 pips. There are 36 possible rolls, which are shown in Table 3-1. There are 21 different moves since many of the rolls, like the 6-2 and 2-6 rolls, provide the same move. The total pips for all 36 possible rolls is 294. This number divided by 36 is 8.17, which is the precise average pips per roll.

Table 3-1

1-1	1-2	1-3	1-4	1-5	1-6
2-1	2-2	2-3	2-4	2-5	2-6
3-1	3-2	3-3	3-4	3-5	3-6
4-1	4-2	4-3	4-4	4-5	4-6
5-1	5-2	5-3	5-4	5-5	5-6
6-1	6-2	6-3	6-4	6-5	6-6

3-20. Number of rolls required to reach inner board is shown in Figure 3-5

As you'll see later, it's important that you always know how many rolls are required to get all of your men into your inner board assuming none of your men are hit. Figure 3-5 shows the method to quickly estimate the number of rolls required to reach your inner board. The

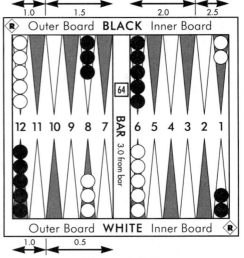

Figure 3-5

resulting estimate is sufficiently accurate. Since the average roll is around 8 pips, men on the 11-point and 12-point require about 1 roll to get into your inner board as shown in Figure 3-5. A man on your opponent's 1-point or 2-point requires about 2.5 rolls. The number of rolls from the other points and the bar are also shown.

For example, if all of your men are in your inner board except for two men on your opponent's 12-point and one man on your 10-point, about 2.5 rolls are required to get all of your men into your inner board so that you can start bearing off.

3-21. If no men are hit or trapped, it usually takes 11.5 rolls to get all men into your inner board

Figure 3-5 shows that it takes around 11.5 rolls from the beginning of a game to get all of a player's men into his inner board if no men are hit or trapped. The men on the opponent's 1-point require 5 rolls, the men on the opponent's 12-point require 5 rolls, and the men on the player's 8-point require 1.5 rolls. Since 11.5 rolls (5 + 5 + 1.5) are required, it's unlikely that a running player will get all of his men into his inner board without having at least one man hit or trapped.

3-22. A running player requires around 21 rolls to win if not hit; around 26 rolls if you hit your opponent twice

You saw that it takes about 11.5 rolls from the beginning of a game to get all of a player's men into his inner board if no men are hit or trapped. It takes about 8 rolls to bear all of the men off if they are evenly distributed in the inner board. Since the first 11.5 rolls won't get the men evenly distributed in the inner board, it will usually take 1.5 extra rolls to bear all of the men off. Therefore, a total of around 21 rolls (11.5 + 8 + 1.5) are required to win if a player's men are not hit or trapped.

You will see later that, in most games, you will hit at least two of the opponent's men. On the average it costs 2.5 rolls each time a man is hit. Thus, your opponent will need about 26 rolls (21 + 2 × 2.5) to win if you hit him twice and he doesn't double you out. If you have one or more men in your opponent's inner board or on the bar, he will need about 1 additional roll to bear his men off safely. And he will need more rolls if you trap one or more of his men or you hit more than two of his men.

HITTING PROBABILITY

It's important that you know the probability of hitting the opponent's men and of being hit to use the correct strategy for moves, doubling, and roll-overs. As you will see in the following chapters, the hitting probability is part of the basics for the correct strategy. You should also use the hitting probabilities to determine the chance of covering a blot with a builder or builders to make a point.

3-23. Chance of hitting a blot is shown in Table 3-2

Table 3-2 shows the number of rolls (out of the 36 possible rolls) that hit and the chance of hitting a blot as a function of the number of points the hitting man (shooter) is from the blot. This table is formed using Table 3-1. For example, looking at the possible rolls in Table 3-1, a blot that is four points away can be hit by the following 15 rolls: 1-1, 2-2, 4-4, 3-1, 1-3, 4-1, 1-4, 4-2, 2-4, 4-3, 3-4, 4-5, 5-4, 4-6, and 6-4. Therefore, the probability of hitting in this case is $^{15}/_{36} = 0.42 = 42\%$. The probability of hitting is by far the highest for a direct shot, where the shooter is six or fewer points from the blot. The highest probability exists when the shooter is six points away. The probability is much less when the shooter is more than six points away (indirect shot), since the right combination of both dice is required to hit. The probability decreases more when the shooter is farther away (except that it's more

Table 3-2

Points away	Rolls that hit	Chance of hitting
1	11	31%
2	12	33%
3	14	39%
4	15	42%
5	15	42%
6	17	47%
7	6	17%
8	6	17%
9	5	14%
10	3	8%
11	2	6%
12	3	8%
16	1	3%
20	1	3%
24	1	3%

likely from 12 points away than 11). This tells you that if you must leave a shot (blot), try to leave it at least seven points from a potential shooter. If you must leave a shot within six points of a potential shooter (direct shot), try to leave it as near to the shooter as possible.

You have a 3 to play in Figure 3-6. You have to leave a direct shot regardless of how you play the 3. The best play is to move a man from your 6-point to your 3-point. If you move a man from your opponent's 12-point to your 10-point instead, that man would be more likely to be hit. The correct move leaves the blot closer to the shooter (one point away instead of five points away).

3-24. Subtract one roll for each intermediate point covered when determining chance of hitting a blot

The probabilities in Table 3-2 assume that the player with the blot owns no points

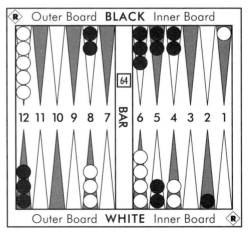

Figure 3-6

between the blot and shooter that interfere with the shot. Usually the player with the blot does own some of the intermediate points. You need to subtract one roll from that shown in Table 3-2 for each intermediate point owned by the opponent to estimate the chance of hitting a blot that is six or fewer points away. For example, a blot that is five points away from your shooter can be hit by 13 rolls (15 − 2) if the opponent owns two intermediate points. In this case you have a 36% ($^{13}/_{36}$) chance of hitting the blot.

3-25. Subtract four rolls after adding chances of two men hitting

When you have two shooters, estimate the number of rolls each shooter has that will hit, then add the rolls together and subtract four to estimate the total rolls that will hit. In Figure 3-7, your man on the opponent's 1-point can hit the blot on the 5-point with 14 rolls (15 − 1) and your man on the 2-point can hit it with 13 rolls (14 − 1). Therefore, you can hit the blot with 23 rolls (14 + 13 − 4), and the chance of hitting is 64% ($^{23}/_{36}$).

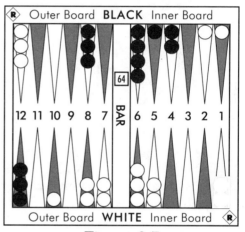

Figure 3-7

3-26. When leaving a shot, try to leave it so it can only be hit by a roll that is good to use elsewhere

You have rolled a 2-1 in Figure 3-8. Your best play is to move a man from your 6-point to your 4-point with the 2, and the man on the 11-point to the 10-point with the 1. With three builders (from your 6-, 8-, and 10-points) to cover your blot on the 4-point, you'll almost certainly make your 4-point on the next roll if the blot isn't hit. This would give you a

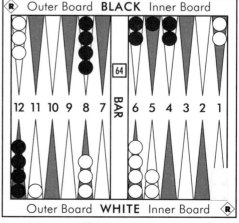

Figure 3-8

four-point blockade. If your opponent rolls a 3 (a 1-1, 2-1, or a 3-n, where n = 1 through 6), which is the roll that can hit your blot, he will have a tough decision. He can either hit your blot with a man from your 1-point or use the 3 to make his 5-point with a man from his 8-point. The 5-point is an important point for him to make, and it would give him a four-point blockade. This is an example of you leaving a constructive shot that can only be hit by a roll that is good to use elsewhere.

If your opponent needs a 4 to make an important point and you have to leave a shot that can be hit either with a 3 or with a 4, leave the shot so that a 4 is required to hit it. If you leave the shot so that a 3 can hit it, then both a 3 and a 4 would be good rolls for your opponent.

3-27. Take risks early before opponent fills his inner board or has strong blockade

Leave blots early in the game, if necessary, to make points between your 3-point and 9-point. Your opponent will probably not own many points in his inner board or have a strong blockade early in the game. If your blot is hit, it will be easy for it to enter and escape early in the game. However, if your opponent owns four or more points in his inner board or has a strong blockade, be more reluctant to leave shots.

You will probably have to take some calculated risks (percentage plays) during a game. You cannot win at backgammon by playing safely all of the time.

4. DOUBLING STRATEGY

In this chapter I will present and explain the basic doubling strategy. This includes when to double, when to accept a double, when to resign, and why, all as a function of your chance of winning the game. In the remaining chapters, I will show you when to double and accept a double during the various phases of a game.

Use of the doubling cube is an integral high-leverage part of the game, so it's essential that you know the correct doubling strategy. It will make or break your success in winning backgammon matches, sessions, and tournaments. If you offer a double at the right time and situation during a game, your opponent has to decide whether to resign and give you the current value of the game or continue and risk twice the points hoping for a favorable change in fortune. You need to know, or at least have a good feel for, the probabilities for rolls, moves, making points, hitting, entering, and bearing off in order to be effective with the doubling cube.

As you will see, at least one double will be offered and a player will resign during most games. This will shorten most games, but there will be many occasions when games are played to completion where a player completes bearing off. These occasions are:
• Neither player acquires a large enough lead to double.
• A player that accepts a double (owns the cube) doesn't achieve a large enough lead to redouble.
• A player is one point from winning the set so the doubling cube cannot be used that game (Crawford Rule).
• Both players are one point from winning the set so there is no sense in doubling.
• A player is playing for a gammon or backgammon.

PRIMARY DOUBLING PRINCIPLES

4-1. Consider doubling with a greater than 62% chance of winning the game

You can consider doubling with a greater than 62% chance of winning the game in order to either win the game without having to play it to completion (your opponent resigns) or double your winnings (your opponent accepts). When you have a substantial lead, you want to win the game immediately without giving your opponent a chance to improve his position and win the game. You want your opponent to pay double (double your winnings) for the chance to improve his fortune in the game if he accepts your double.

At first glance you might think to double as soon as you have more than a 50% chance of winning the game. This would be foolish since your opponent would gladly accept your double, own the cube, and look to double you out later in the game. The key rule here is that when a player accepts a double, he owns the cube and only he can offer the next double. Once you double and give the cube to your opponent, you cannot double again unless your opponent has subsequently doubled you. If your opponent owns the cube, you cannot double him out even if you have reached a high chance of winning the game. This gives your opponent a chance to get lucky and win.

The magic 62% number is obtained by using the following logic. If you have a 62% chance of winning when you double, you will need to improve your game by 38% (100 − 62) to 100% to win, since your opponent will own the cube. As you will see in the next doubling principle, a player should resign if he has less than a 25% chance of winning the game. Therefore, your opponent, who has a 38% (100 − 62) chance of winning, also needs to improve his game by 38% (76 − 38) to 76% to win, since he will double you out if he reaches a 76% chance of winning the game. Thus, the break-even point occurs when you have a 62% chance of winning the game since both you and your opponent need to improve your game by 38% from that point to win. If you have more than a 62% chance of winning, you can consider doubling. If you have less than a 62% chance, don't.

The difficult part is knowing your chance of winning the game at each roll during the game. Throughout the rest of this book I will give you methods for determining your chance of winning. This is an important and difficult aspect of the game. There is plenty of room for you to improve your doubling ability, particularly during the midgame phase, through playing experience and studying the game.

4-2. Accept double with a greater than 25% chance of winning the game

This doubling principle can be easily seen by looking at a four game series in which you are doubled each game. If you resign in each game, you lose 4 points since a basic game is worth 1 point. If you accept the double in each game and win one of the four games, you lose 4 points also $(6 - 2)$. In this case you lose 6 points for the three double games that you lose and win 2 points for the double game you win for a net loss of 4 points. Therefore, the break-even point occurs when you can win one of the four games; in other words, when you have a 25% chance of winning the game. If you have more than a 25% chance of winning the game, accept the double assuming your chance of being gammoned is small. With less of a chance, resign. In both cases you will probably lose points since you have much less than a 50% chance of winning, but you will minimize your losses when you have between a 25% and 50% chance of winning if you accept the double. If you have more than a 50% chance of winning, you will double your winnings and it is clear that your opponent shouldn't have doubled.

To illustrate this principle, assume that you win three of ten games (30% chance of winning) and your opponent doubles you in each game. If you resign every game, you will lose 10 points. If you accept each double, you will lose only 8 points $(14 - 6)$, a difference of 2 points! The difference would be 10 points if you win five of the games (50% chance of winning)! However, if you win only two of the ten games (20% chance of winning) and accept each double, you will lose 12 points $(16 - 4)$, which is a loss of 2 more points than if you had resigned every game.

Since a player can consider doubling when he reaches a greater than 62% chance of winning the game and a player should accept a double when he has more than a 25% chance of winning the game, there is a 13% region $(75 - 62)$ where a double can be made and accepted. When two players that use the correct doubling strategy are playing each other, most doubles will be accepted.

If there is a decent (more than 15%) chance that you will be gammoned, you need significantly more than a 25% chance (several percent more) of winning the game to accept a double.

4-3. Early in a game, accept double with less than a 25% chance of winning game (around 22%) since you only need to achieve a 76% chance of winning in one of four games to win one of four games

This is a fine point, but it's worth knowing. If you are doubled early in the game, accept with just a 22% chance of winning the game. In this case, you have more time to improve your chance of winning to 76% to double your opponent out in 25% of these games. You may not have to improve your chance of winning to 100%. Realizing that this is a somewhat infrequent and small exception, the basic doubling

principles are summarized in
Table 4-1.

Table 4-1

Chance of winning	Doubling strategy
0% to 25%	Resign double
26% to 100%	Accept double
63% to 100%	Consider doubling
75% to 100%	Expect opponent to resign

4-4. Optimum time to double occurs when you have the highest chance of winning the game and your opponent will still accept

You can consider doubling when you have more than a 62% chance of winning the game. You want to double when you have the highest chance of winning and your opponent will still accept your double. This maximizes the points that you'll win. If your chance of winning is unlikely to increase in the next round to the point that your opponent will resign, wait at least one round to double.

On the other hand, if your lead is so large that your opponent would certainly decline your double and you are unlikely to lose a lot of your lead in the next round, wait at least one round to double. If your lead decreases to the point that your opponent is likely to accept, double then.

4-5. Doubling range as function of opponent's acceptance point is shown in Table 4-2

You need to have a good idea of the chance-of-winning point that your opponent will no longer accept a double. You learned that this should be 25% (75% chance of winning for the doubler). Since, in most situations, you cannot precisely determine your chance

Table 4-2

Opponent acceptance pt.	Doubling range
30%	65%-75%
25%	70%-80%
20%	75%-85%

of winning or know your opponent's double-acceptance point with certainty, there is a chance-of-winning range in which the right thing to do is double. This range will vary with your opponent's double-acceptance point as shown in Table 4-2. For example, if your opponent usually wants to have at least a 30% chance of winning to accept a double, double if you have between a 65% and 75% chance of winning the game. In this case, wait to double if you have more than a 75% of winning because your opponent will probably resign. You will learn in Chapter 11 that a player's double-acceptance point will vary depending on whether he is ahead or behind in a set.

If your opponent uses the correct double-acceptance point (25%), a double when you have an 80% chance of winning (opponent resigns) is just as effective in winning points as a double when you have a 70% chance of winning (opponent accepts). The optimum time to double in this case is when you have a 75% chance of winning the game.

When you own the doubling cube (rather than it being on the middle of the bar), wait to double until you have a few percent (2 or 3) higher chance of winning than normal. The cube is more valuable to you when you own it so be more reluctant to give it to your opponent.

DOUBLING SITUATIONS

If you are going to double, you must offer the double when it is your turn before you roll the dice. As a result, you need to quickly update your assessment of your chance of winning before you roll each turn. This will also enable you to quickly decide whether to accept if your opponent doubles.

4-6. Consider doubling if two or more rolls ahead with one or more opponent men trapped behind blockade of four or more points

This is a good rule of thumb for doubling that you can use to quickly assess your chance of winning. It's amazingly accurate in telling you whether you have more than a 62% chance of winning the game. If you have one or more men trapped, though, don't consider doubling.

In Figure 4-1, you have the minimum lead to consider doubling. You have a 63% chance of winning the game. Using the method that you learned earlier, you can quickly count that you are 8 rolls from having all of your men in your inner board. Your opponent is 10 rolls from having all of his men in his inner board so you have a 2-roll lead. You have one of your opponent's men trapped behind your four-point blockade, and your opponent doesn't have a four-point blockade to trap your man. If you had any smaller lead, you wouldn't consider doubling. Of course, you should also consider doubling with a larger

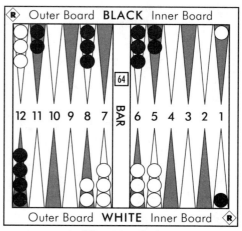

Figure 4-1

lead, if, for example, you have more than a 2-roll lead, you have more men trapped, or you have a bigger blockade.

Table 4-3

Rolls ahead	Blockade points	Men trapped	Chance of winning
2	4	1	63%
2	4	2	70%
2	5	1	70%
2	5	2	75%
3	<4	0	70%
3	4	1	73%
3	4	2	75%
3	5	1	75%
3	5	2	80%

4-7. Chance of winning game is shown in Table 4-3

The approximate chance of winning the game as a function of your lead, number of points in your blockade, and number of men that you have trapped is shown in Table 4-3. The actual chance of winning will vary depending on other factors such as the number of blots each player has and whether you have a man trapped. Adjust the chance of winning by around 2% for each extra blot that can be hit, and reduce it by about 8% if you have a man trapped behind a four-point or five-point blockade. Use this information in combination with Table 4-2 in deciding whether to double. For example, double if your opponent uses the correct double-acceptance point, you have a 3-roll lead, you have one of the opponent's men trapped behind your four-point blockade, and you don't have any men trapped. Use Table 4-3 in deciding whether to accept a double as well.

4-8. In straight race, consider doubling when greater than 5% ahead in pips with distribution equal to opponent; accept double if less than (5% + 3) pips behind

It's your turn in Figure 4-2 and you are in a straight race since your men are no longer in contact (interlocked) with your opponent's. In a straight race, you and your opponent can no longer hit each other's men, so the game is now simply a race to bear off all of your men first. In this example, you and your opponent

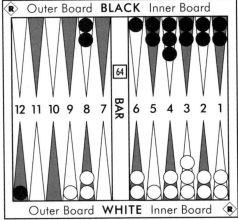

Figure 4-2

40

have an equal and nearly even distribution of men in your inner boards. You will see in Chapter 8 that your pip count is approximately 54 when all of your men are in your inner board evenly distributed. In other words, you have to move your men a total of approximately 54 pips to bear them completely off when all of your men are in your inner board evenly distributed.

In Figure 4-2, you are 1.5 rolls (12 pips since 1 roll is equal to 8 pips) from having all of your men evenly distributed in your inner board. Therefore, your total pip count is about 66 pips (12 + 54). Your opponent is 2 rolls from having all of his men evenly distributed in his inner board so his total pip count is around 70 pips (16 + 54). Your lead in the race is about 4 pips or approximately 6% (4/66). Since your lead is more than 5% of the pips and your distribution is equal to your opponent's, seriously consider doubling. You have more than a 69% chance of winning the game. Your opponent should accept if you double because you have less than a 75% chance of winning the game.

If your lead were (5% + 3) pips, which is 7 pips in this example, you would have around a 77% chance of winning, you would definitely double, and your opponent should resign.

4-9. Double when opponent is trapped behind your prime unless you have good chance for gammon

Black has doubled in Figure 4-3 (see front cover). When you first look at the situation, you might conclude that black has an insurmountable lead and white should resign. Actually, white can double black out because white has black trapped behind a prime. Black has to move men forward in his inner board, which will break his prime. White cannot enter his man or move until black breaks his prime. This and many other situations included in this book illustrate how important it is to know and use the correct strategy.

You learned earlier that you have a greater than 95% chance of winning the game

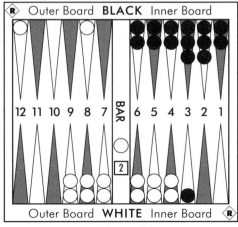

Figure 4-3

when you have one or more of the opponent's men trapped behind your prime, if you don't have men trapped such that you would have to break your prime before you get them freed. Therefore, consider doubling as soon as you have your opponent trapped behind your prime unless you have men dangerously trapped or you have a good chance for winning a gammon. You will learn later that you usually have a good chance of winning a gammon when you have three or more men trapped behind your prime. In that case continue playing, rather than double, as long as your gammon chance remains good.

If you're sure that your chance of winning won't drop to less than 70% in the next round, wait at least one round before doubling to try to get your opponent to accept your double.

4-10. Double when you get 3 rolls ahead unless you have a man trapped, opponent has a strong blockade, or you have more than one blot in danger; it takes only a 2-roll lead if it is likely that you will become uninterlocked without getting hit

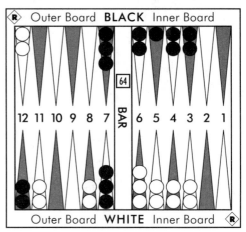

Figure 4-4

In Figure 4-4, it's your turn and you should double even though you don't have any of the opponent's men trapped. You have a 3-roll lead (your opponent is 8 rolls and you are 5 rolls from having all men in your inner boards), which is large enough to give you about a 70% chance of winning the game (see Table 4-3). You don't have any men trapped and your opponent's blockade isn't strong. Your opponent should accept your double. If you were less interlocked so that it would be easier to turn the game into a straight race, you should double with only a 2-roll lead.

OTHER DOUBLING CONSIDERATIONS

4-11. Usually double if opponent has a large flaw in his position

If your opponent has a large flaw in his position, you have a small roll lead, and you don't have any men trapped, it's usually the right move

to double. Large position flaws include any of the following:
• Your opponent has more than two men on his 1-point or 2-point early in the game.
• Your opponent has more than six men on a point unless he is getting all of his men into his inner board to start bearing off.
• Your opponent has more than three blots that you can hit and would like to hit.
• Your opponent has more than four men in your inner board.

4-12. Do not double when you have a reasonable (more than 50%) chance of winning gammon

If you have a reasonable (more than 50%) chance of winning a gammon, continue trying for the gammon rather than double. If your chance for the gammon decreases, double if you still have a large enough chance of winning the game. If your chance of winning a gammon is greater than 50%, your opponent will probably gladly resign if you double. It's worth the risk to try for the gammon in this case, which would give you twice the current value of the game, than to double and receive only the current value of the game.

Actually, this case will not occur often because you should double when you reach about 70% chance of winning the game. This case will occur if your fortunes increase from less than a 70% chance of winning the game to more than a 50% chance of winning a gammon in one round. One way that this can occur is when you complete a prime trapping three or more of the opponent's men.

4-13. To gammon opponent, you usually have to trap three or more men behind a prime; then chance is around 60% for gammon

Your chance of winning a gammon is around 60% when you have three or more of the opponent's men trapped behind your prime. By the time you have to break your prime and all of the opponent's men have escaped, you'll probably have most of your men borne off if none of

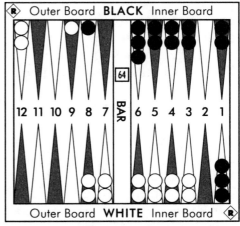

Figure 4-5

them get hit. This shows you that it is fairly hard to gammon a good opponent, but you can often gammon an inexperienced player.

In Figure 4-5, you have just completed your prime with three of your opponent's men trapped behind it. Continue the game trying to win a gammon instead of doubling.

There are, of course, other ways to win a gammon. One way occurs when your opponent is playing a back game and fails to hit you. In fact, you can win a backgammon if your opponent is playing an all-out back game and fails to hit you.

4-14. Usually resign when more than 3 rolls behind

Generally, resign a double if you are more than 3 rolls behind, unless you have one or more of your opponent's men trapped. This can be seen by extrapolating in Table 4-3. If you are more than 3 rolls behind, you have too much ground to make up and have less than a 25% chance of winning the game, unless it's early in the game.

An obvious exception is when you have your opponent trapped behind a prime. In this case you have more than a 95% chance of winning the game if you are in no danger of having to break your prime, regardless of how many rolls you are behind. You are the player that should double rather than your opponent!

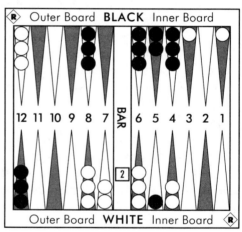

Figure 4-6

In Figure 4-6, it's your opponent's turn and he has offered a double. You are 3.5 rolls (10 – 6.5) behind and ought to resign.

4-15. Double earlier than usual when playing a less experienced player

When you're playing a less experienced player, your lead in the game is more likely to increase than decrease. Thus, double with a smaller chance of winning than usual to increase the likelihood that he will accept and increase the points that you win. You will win a high percentage of the games and win fairly frequent gammons. If this is the case, introduce your opponent to this book so that he can become a more challenging player.

4-16. Often one player can double by his seventh roll

In many games, you or your opponent can double by the seventh round. This shows that the first few moves are important, and a player can achieve a large enough chance of winning the game to double fairly quickly. Most likely, though, the other player should accept the double so the first seven rolls are seldom "do or die."

4-17. With two good players, the cube does not reach 8 often; most games it is 1 or 2; some games it becomes 4

Although the lead can change hands quickly and often in backgammon, making it an exciting game, a player's chance of winning does not change from between 70% and 75% to between 25% and 30% (or vice versa) often in a game. When two good players that know the correct doubling strategy are playing, the cube will be at only 1 or 2 in most games. The cube will become 4 (two doubles are accepted) in a number of games, but it won't reach 8 often. Thus, the game value will be 1 or 2, maybe 4, points in almost all games. Occasional gammons and backgammons, of course, will increase the game value.

5. ROLL-OVER STRATEGY

The roll-over is a variant that I highly recommend be used because it adds strategy, reduces the element of luck, and reduces frustration. It adds a worthwhile, interesting aspect and enhances the quality of the game. There are times when a player is quite glad to erase a devastatingly unlucky roll. You need to obtain agreement from your opponent as well as every player in a tournament to use the roll-over. If you use the correct roll-over strategy, it can be an effective weapon and can reduce frustration.

BASIC ROLL-OVER STRATEGY

5-1. Do not let frustration or emotions determine when you use your roll-over

You will be tempted to use your roll-over every time you become frustrated by bad luck in a game. While the roll-over can reduce frustration by erasing really bad luck, you must not let emotions alone determine when you use it. Correct use of the roll-over will significantly increase your chance of winning.

5-2. Use roll-over when:
* *Opponent gets a 1-in-18 (or 1-in-36) roll that really hurts*
* *Opponent gets a roll that will allow him to double you out*
* *Your roll allows opponent to double you out*
* *You have more than a 70% chance of putting opponent in deep hole and miss it*
* *Opponent rolls double 4s, 5s, or 6s in a straight race*
* *You do not bear at least two men off with just a couple rolls left in game*
* *Opponent bears off more than two men with just a couple rolls left in game*

Since there are 36 possible rolls, a player has a 1-in-36 chance of rolling a particular doubles, such as 4-4. A player has a 1-in-18 (2-in-36) chance of rolling a specific combination such as 5-2 (or 2-5). In some games your opponent will get a 1-in-18 roll that really hurts; that is, it suddenly puts him considerably ahead or erases your big lead.

This is the time to use your roll-over.

In Figure 5-1, your opponent has just rolled a 6-1 that really stings. You have the opponent's man badly trapped and this 1-in-18 roll is the only roll that allows the man to escape. You nearly have a large enough lead to double and you are close to having a prime in front of the opponent's man, but this lucky roll foils your position. This is an example of a good time to use your roll-over to have your opponent roll again and keep his man trapped. If the man escapes, the game is pretty much even. If you can keep the man trapped, you'll most likely win the game.

In Figure 5-2, you have hit your opponent's blot that was on your 8-point and are on the way to a certain win and possible gammon. Incredibly, your opponent has just rolled a lucky 4-4. This 1-in-36 roll will allow your opponent to enter and escape with his man from the bar, hit your blot, and make his 4-point putting your hit man on the bar behind a five-point blockade. This roll would completely distort the game turning your large lead into a large lead for your opponent. Quickly and gladly use your roll-over to erase this devastating roll. Lucky rolls like this illustrate

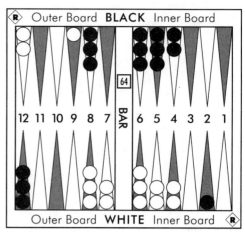

Figure 5-1

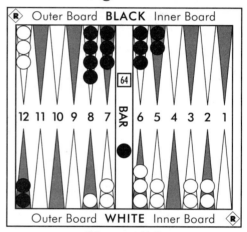

Figure 5-2

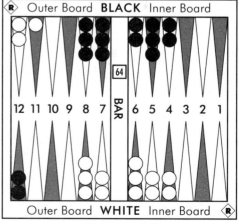

Figure 5-3

the essence of the roll-over. Your opponent cannot use his roll-over to restore his 4-4 roll. He can only use his roll-over to cause his reroll or any future roll to be rolled again.

In Figure 5-3, your opponent has rolled a 5-2, which hits your blot. This will allow your opponent to double you out the next turn because you will be 2.5 rolls behind with a man trapped behind a five-point blockade late in the

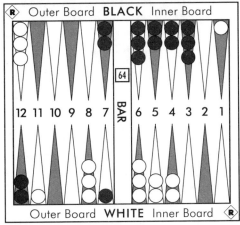

Figure 5-4

game. It's clear that you must use your roll-over to avoid being doubled out. If your blot isn't hit, you're still behind, but you have a chance to catch up.

In Figure 5-4, you have just rolled a unfortunate 3-2. This roll, 5-3, and 5-2 are the only rolls that will allow your opponent to double you out. A 5-5 would reduce the lead enough not to be doubled out and every other roll hits your opponent's blot. If you hit the blot, you will still be behind, but you avoid being doubled out. You must use your roll-over to keep your unlucky roll from allowing your opponent to double you out.

In Figure 5-5, you have rolled a 5-2, which is one of the few rolls that doesn't hit either blot in your opponent's boards. If you hit one of those blots, you can double on your next turn and your opponent will probably resign. Use your roll-over since you have greater than a 70% chance of hitting one of the blots, which would put your opponent in a deep hole.

In Figure 5-6, you have around a 70% chance of completing your prime since any 2 or 6 will do it. If you complete your prime, you'll have more than a 95% chance of winning and can double your opponent out. If you don't cover your blot completing

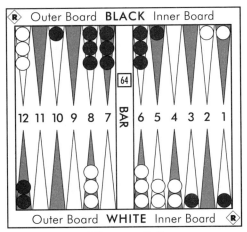

Figure 5-5

your prime, your opponent can hit it and possibly escape, giving him a large lead. So, use your roll-over if you don't get a roll that completes your prime.

When you're in a straight race and you haven't already used your roll-over, use it if your opponent rolls double 4s, 5s, or 6s. Since the average roll is 8 pips, these rolls are well above average and are damaging in a race.

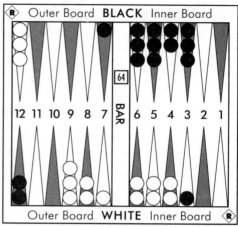

Figure 5-6

If you still have your roll-over with only a couple rolls left in bearing men off, use it if you get a roll that doesn't bear at least two men off, or if your opponent gets a roll that bears off more than two men.

5-3. If you have your roll-over, you can take a risk to put your opponent in a deep hole

In Figure 5-7, you have rolled a 4-1. Move a man from your 7-point to your 6-point, and take a risk by moving a man from your opponent's 12-point to your 9-point. This will make it likely that you will complete a prime next roll by making your 3-point or 9-point. This would give you about a 95% chance of winning the game. If your opponent gets lucky and rolls the disastrous 6-2 (1-in-18) roll, you will have him roll over. If you didn't have your roll-over, his 6-2 roll would put two or three of your blots on the bar behind his prime and he would likely win a gammon.

OTHER ROLL-OVER CONSIDERATIONS

You are making optimum use of your roll-over if you use it in every game, and use it for the most unfortunate roll in each game. Naturally, you

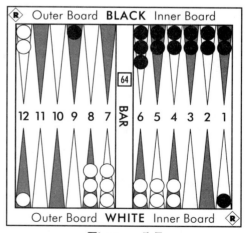

Figure 5-7

50

don't need to use it when you maintain a substantial lead throughout games you win. There is no way that you can guarantee optimum use. However, using the roll-over strategy that you have just learned, along with experience, will result in near optimum use of the roll-over.

5-4. In over 80% of games a player is doubled out, so less than 20% of games are won by completely bearing off

While you shouldn't let your emotions tempt you to use your roll-over for every unlucky roll, you shouldn't save it too long, either. You should and usually will use your roll-over before you are doubled out. When your opponent is an equally good player, you'll be doubled out in more than 40% of the games because one player or the other is doubled out in more than 80% of the games. Since less than 20% of the games are won by completely bearing off, you should normally use your roll-over before the game becomes a straight race.

5-5. In more than 60% of games the players are still interlocked when one of them is doubled out

This is another principle that helps give you a better feel for both the doubling and roll-over strategies. This shows you that less than 40% of the games become a straight race. In most games, you will double and use your roll-over before the game becomes a straight race. But don't panic if the game is becoming a straight race and you haven't used your roll-over. This probably means you haven't had any really bad luck in the game. There is still time for you or your opponent to make a roll that is quite unfortunate for you.

5-6. In only around 15% of games do the players become uninterlocked without a double

This is similar to the previous principle. It tells you that a double is almost a certainty, and that you will usually use your roll-over before the game becomes a straight race. There is a good chance that your opponent will roll double 4s or better in a race. If you still have your roll-over when the game becomes a straight race, save it for this unfortunate occurrence.

5-7. Consider the roll-over in conjunction with doubling strategy

You always need to take the roll-over situation into account when deciding whether to double and whether to accept a double.

Your opponent has doubled in Figure 5-8. He has a speed board and will certainly win the game if his man on your 4-point escapes this roll. If the man doesn't escape, you will most likely hit it and his chance of winning the game will be substantially reduced. Your only roll that wouldn't substantially reduce your opponent's lead is 6-5. You have used your roll-over and your opponent still has his.

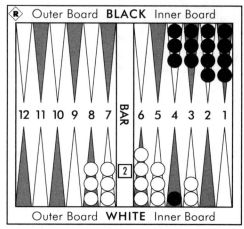

Figure 5-8

Since he will certainly use his roll-over if he doesn't escape, he has two rolls to roll a 5 or 6 to escape. You will see later in Chapter 7 that he has a 56% chance of rolling a 5 or 6 in one roll and an 80% chance in two rolls. Therefore, he basically has an 80% chance of winning the game considering his roll-over, so you should resign. You could accept the double if he didn't have his roll-over or if you still had yours. Your opponent shouldn't double in this situation if you still have your roll-over since you will have him roll again if he escapes.

5-8. Roll-over is worth approximately 4% game or approximately 7% pips in a straight race

When you still have your roll-over and your opponent has used his, you have an extra 4% or so chance of winning the game, or an extra 7% or so pip lead in a straight race. Similarly, your opponent has the same extra lead (or you have a lesser lead) when you have used your roll-over and your opponent still has his. You have to take this into account when you assess your chance of winning the game for doubling and accepting a double. This indicates that the roll-over is significant, but not a

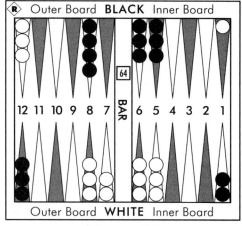

Figure 5-9

large factor, for two players that use the correct roll-over strategy. The roll-over doesn't represent a significant difference in the chance of winning when both players or neither player has his roll-over and both players know how to use the roll-over effectively.

It's your turn in Figure 5-9 and you have around a 71% chance of winning the game before the roll-over is considered. If you still had your roll-over, you could double. Since you have used your roll-over and your opponent still has his, you have only around a 67% (71 − 4) chance of winning and shouldn't double.

In Figure 5-10 it is your turn and you have about a 68% chance of winning the game before taking into account the roll-over. Since you still have your roll-over and your opponent has used his, you have around a 72% (68 + 4) chance of winning

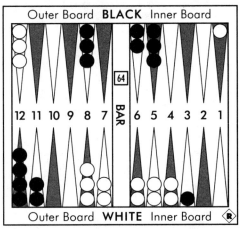

Figure 5-10

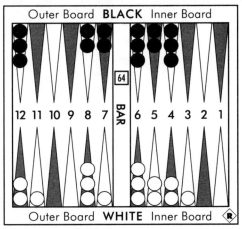

Figure 5-11

and should double. Your opponent should accept your double.

You're nearly even in the race in Figure 5-11. Your opponent has used his roll-over, but you still have yours and it is your turn. The roll-over is worth about 7% pips in a race so you should double (see Principle 4-8). Your opponent should accept.

6. OPENING AND EARLY-GAME MOVES

The opening and early moves in a game are important because they set the stage for the rest of the game. If you use the correct opening and early moves, you will usually build a blockade, gain a lead, and win the game and possibly a gammon. On the other hand, if you get off on the wrong foot, it's usually difficult to recover. In many of those games, however, you can come back and win if you use the correct strategy. Never throw in the towel unless it's right to decline your opponent's double.

You have learned that one of the players can often double by his seventh roll of a game. In more than 60% of the games, the players are still interlocked when one of them is doubled out. These facts emphasize the importance of the opening and early-game moves.

These moves are like initial ball possession in a football game. The receiving team wants to return the opening kickoff to get good field position and score on the first drive to put themselves in a strong position early in the game (like building a good blockade quickly).

OPENING MOVES

Since a blocking game is superior to a running game, the best opening moves are the ones that start building your blockade between your 3-point and 9-point. The opening moves that I recommend should be used for your first move, or first few moves, of each game and provide good guidance for subsequent moves.

6-1. Best opening moves:
- *1-1: make 5-point and 7-point*
- *2-2: make 4-point and 11-point*
- *3-3: make 5-point and 3-point*
- *4-4: make 5-point*
- *5-5: make 3-point*
- *6-6: make both 7-points*
- *3-1: make 5-point*

- *6-1: make 7-point*
- *4-2: make 4-point*
- *6-5, 6-4, and 6-3: move runner*
- *5-3: move two men to outer board; if opponent has split runners, make 3-point*
- *6-2: move runner with 6 and man to 11-point with 2*
- *2-1, 4-1, and 5-1: move man to outer board and use 1 to split runners*
- *3-2, 4-3, 5-2, and 5-4: move two men to outer board*

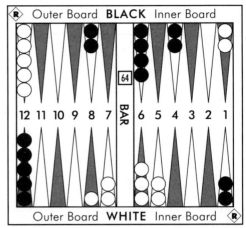

Figure 6-1

This principle gives you the best opening move for each of the 36 possible rolls (21 possible moves). The opening move for each double is shown first, followed by the opening move for the other rolls. The doubles, 3-1, 6-1, 4-2, and 6-5 are all really good opening rolls. Some of the other rolls can also be good if you make the correct move and have a little luck. Doubles are not possible for the first roll of a game, but they are possible for all subsequent rolls. For this reason, winning the opening move can be a disadvantage for some of the rolls.

1-1: Make your 5-point and 7-point as shown in Figure 6-1. Move two men from your 6-point and two men from your 8-point. This is by far the best way to use this excellent roll. The blot you leave on your 8-point is fairly safe. You can cover it with any 5 move to quickly establish a four-point blockade. I won't illustrate the other opening moves with a figure since they should be easy to understand. You should perform each of the opening moves with your backgammon set to help you remember them.

2-2: Make your 4-point and 11-point. Move two men from your 6-point to 4-point, and two men from your opponent's 12-point to your 11-point. This makes a point for your blockade in your inner board and brings some builders safely into position to make more points in your blockade.

3-3: Make your 5-point and 3-point. Move two men from your 8-point and two men from your 6-point. It's worth giving up your 8-point temporarily to make these two important inner board points. Like with a 1-1, the blot you leave on your 8-point is fairly safe.

4-4: Make your 5-point by moving two men from your opponent's 12-point to your 9-point and then to your 5-point. You might want to make your opponent's 5-point and your own 9-point with this roll. It's much more beneficial, however, to make your 5-point instead of your opponent's 5-point. Your 5-point is part of your blockade, makes it more difficult for your opponent to enter men, and will be held until you are bearing men off. You would only be holding your opponent's 5-point temporarily.

5-5: Make your 3-point by moving two men from your opponent's 12-point to your 8-point and then to your 3-point. It's good to make your 3-point since it's the third point of your blockade and is in your inner board. But avoid putting any more men on your 3-point early in the game because that would put them too far advanced to be effective.

6-6: Make your 7-point and your opponent's 7-point. Move two men from your opponent's 12-point to your 7-point, and your runners to your opponent's 7-point. This roll makes a point in your blockade, safely advances your runners, and moves your men 24 pips in the race.

3-1: Make your 5-point by moving one man from your 8-point and one from your 6-point. This is the best initial roll of a game that you can get since the doubles aren't possible for the initial roll.

6-1: Make your 7-point by moving one man from your opponent's 12-point and one from your 8-point. This makes the third point of your blockade.

4-2: Make your 4-point by moving a man from your 8-point and from your 6-point.

6-5, 6-4, and 6-3: Move one of your runners with these opening rolls. The 6-5 gets one of your runners to safety on your opponent's 12-point. The 6-4 and 6-3 leave a blot in your opponent's outer board, but this is the best way to play these rolls. Do not move a man to your outer board with the 3 and a runner to your opponent's 7-point with the 6. This puts the runner in too much danger.

5-3: Move two men to your outer board. Move a man from your opponent's 12-point to your 8-point, and a man from your opponent's

12-point to your 10-point. If your opponent has split his runners, make your 3-point by moving a man from your 8-point and a man from your 6-point. You might see a player move a man from his opponent's 12-point to his own 5-point (called slotting the 5-point) for this roll. Although this provides a chance to make the important 5-point, it's just too risky. The blot on the 5-point has a good chance of being hit, and you lose too much if it is. Your chance of winning the game is low if the blot is hit. It's better to make your 5-point in a safer manner. Avoid getting into an unfavorable hitting war where your men get hit in your inner board.

6-2: Move a runner to your opponent's 7-point and a man from your opponent's 12-point to your 11-point. This puts your runner in jeopardy, but it makes it dangerous for your opponent to put a blot in his outer board and provides a builder on your 11-point for your blockade. An alternate move for this poor roll, which is nearly as good, is to move your runner to your opponent's 9-point. This still puts your runner in danger, though, and doesn't provide a builder for your blockade. Again, you might see a player slot the 5-point for this roll. As explained above, this is just too risky.

2-1, 4-1, and 5-1: Move a man from your opponent's 12-point to your outer board and move a runner to your opponent's 2-point. This provides a builder in your outer board for your blockade. Your runners are still safe and your chance of hitting a blot in your opponent's inner and outer boards is nearly doubled. This also makes it somewhat easier for your runners to escape later, or to make your opponent's 4-, 5-, or 7-point. Your opponent does not want to move men to his 1-point or 2-point early in the game. Don't use the 1 to move a man from your 6-point to your 5-point.

3-2, 4-3, 5-2, and 5-4: Move two men to your outer board from your opponent's 12-point with these rolls. This provides two builders for your blockade that are fairly safe. Don't use the 4 to move your runner to your opponent's 5-point. Although this makes it dangerous for your opponent to put blots in his outer board, it's too risky and does not help build your blockade. This blot is too likely to get hit, which would slow your progress too much.

In Figure 6-2, your opponent has won the opening roll with a 6-1 and has correctly made his 7-point. You have rolled a 6-6 for your opening move. Since your opponent has made his 7-point, you cannot make the normal move of making both 7-points, so this large roll turns out to be a poor one. There are three potential ways to play this roll. All of them make your 7-point, which is the only good news. The least attractive option is to move two men from your opponent's 12-point to your 7-point and two men from your 8-point to your 2-point. This gets two men too far advanced, breaks your 8-point, and leaves a blot on your 8-point. A better option is to

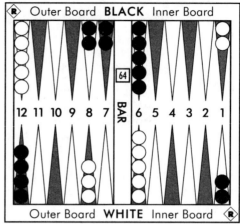

Outer Board **BLACK** Inner Board

12 11 10 9 8 7 | BAR | 6 5 4 3 2 1

Outer Board **WHITE** Inner Board

Figure 6-2

move four men from your opponent's 12-point to your 7-point. This breaks the 12-point and leaves a blot there. The best option, the play to make, is to move three men from your opponent's 12-point to your 7-point and one man from your 8-point to your 2-point. This keeps your points intact and advances only one man too far. It leaves a blot on your 2-point, which is bad, but this is the least of the evils. If the blot is hit, at least it's back in play.

EARLY-GAME MOVES AND STRATEGY

6-2. Generally better to make your 5-point than to hit; otherwise, hit

If you get a roll that can either make your 5-point or hit an opponent's blot in an outer board, make your 5-point. Don't hit a blot in your inner board unless you can point on it (make the point so you don't leave a blot). It's too risky to leave a blot in your inner board. In virtually all other situations, hit a blot if you can. You will gain a substantial lead if you can hit a blot in your opponent's inner board. This is a good principle throughout the game, not just in the early game.

By hitting a blot you set your opponent back in the race, make him use half of his next roll to enter the man, and often trap the man. Also, it might take your opponent two or more rolls to enter the man.

You have rolled a 4-2 in Figure 6-3. Point on the blot on your 4-point by moving a man from your 8-point and 6-point rather than making your 5-point (from your 9-point and 7-point). Although the 4-point isn't quite as valuable as the 5-point, you gain more by hitting the blot.

6-3. Be reluctant to leave a blot in your inner board

Be reluctant to leave a blot in your inner board, particularly if your opponent has a man in your inner board or on the bar to hit it. Be careful in leaving a blot in your inner board even if your opponent doesn't have a man in position to hit it. You might hit an opponent's man, putting it on the bar

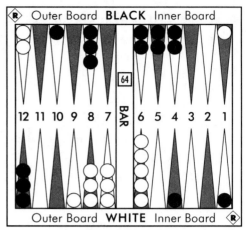

Figure 6-3

and putting your blot in danger. Although putting a blot in your inner board increases your chance of making an important point, it's generally too risky. The blot has a good chance of being hit, and you lose too much (around 3 rolls) if it's hit. Your chance of winning the game is greatly reduced if the blot is hit. It's better to make your inner board points with a roll that moves two men to the point, making the point.

6-4. When determining best move, compare "net positive" of each alternative where "net positive" is number of rolls that will make an important point next move minus number of opponent's rolls that will hit you

The net positive should be 18 or more to leave a blot in your inner board or 7-point if you don't have a better move. It can be much less for the other points in your outer board.

You rolled a 5-2 in Figure 6-4, moved a man from your opponent's 12-point to your 8-point with the 5, and are considering putting a blot on your 4-point from the 6-point as shown. You have no good move for the 5-2 roll. If the blot isn't hit and you cover it, you'll have a good four-point blockade. From Table 3-2, you

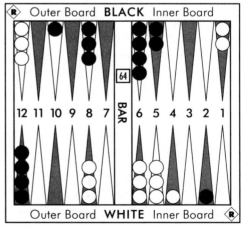

Figure 6-4

can see that 12 of the 36 rolls will hit your blot. If the blot isn't hit, then only 6 rolls (5-3, 3-5, 5-5, 6-5, 5-6, 6-6) won't cover it. Since 30 rolls will cover the blot and 12 rolls will hit it, the net positive is 18. Therefore, it's acceptable (just barely) to put the blot on your 4-point in this situation.

6-5. Split runners with a 1 or 2 roll if there is no other beneficial way of using it

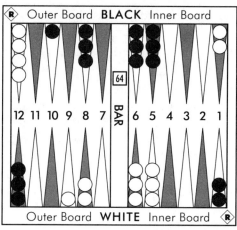

Figure 6-5

In Figure 6-5, you have rolled a 4-1. Use the 4 to move a man from your opponent's 12-point to make your 9-point. There is no constructive way to use the 1 to improve your blockade so use it to split your runners by moving a runner from your opponent's 1-point to 2-point. Actually, splitting your runners with a 1 is an effective move. Your runners are still safe and your chance of hitting a blot in your opponent's inner and outer boards is almost doubled. This also makes it somewhat easier for your runners to escape later. Your opponent doesn't want to move men to his 1-point or 2-point early in the game. Splitting your runners with a 2 is as effective, but your runner on the opponent's 3-point is much more likely to be hit. Don't split your runners with a 3 or 4 because a blot on your opponent's 4-point or 5-point is likely to be hit.

6-6. Do not make your 1-point or 2-point too early. This puts men out of play, makes it difficult to build a side prime, and wastes pips in being able to start bearing off

Your 1-point and 2-point are too far advanced to put your men on them early in a game. The last thing you want to do is put a blot on your 1-point or 2-point early in the game. These points wouldn't contribute to a blockade or side prime. Men on these points would no longer serve as shooters to hit your opponent's men, and would be farther advanced than necessary to allow you to start bearing men off. The only way a man on your 1-point or 2-point can get back into play is by being hit. Also, don't put a third man on your 3-point after you make it early in a game for the same reasons.

6-7. If you roll 6-6 early, your priority should shift toward a running game

If you roll a 6-6 early in a game and can use all of the roll, your strategy should shift toward a running game. Although a blocking game is superior to a running game, a 6-6 roll will probably give you a big lead that you should take advantage of. Give priority to bringing your runners to safety and making inner board points, even your 1-point and 2-point, to get all of your men into your inner board and win the race.

6-8. If your opponent has blots on your 1-point and 3-points and you roll 5-5 early in a game, play a wipeout game by making your 1-point and 3-point, hitting both blots

You have rolled a 5-5 in Figure 6-6. Play a wipeout game by moving two men from your 8-point to your 3-point and two men from your 6-point to your 1-point, hitting both of your opponent's blots. This makes four of your inner board points with two of the opponent's men on the bar. You will probably be able to detain at least one of the opponent's men long enough to give you an insurmountable lead. Even

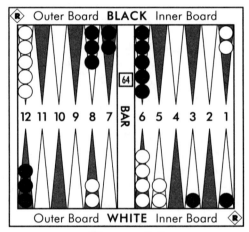

Figure 6-6

if you hadn't made your 5-point, playing a wipeout game in this situation is the way to go. Often, a wipeout game will yield a gammon.

There are many similar situations early in a game where you should put two of the opponent's men on the bar, quickly make your inner board points, and win a gammon.

7. MID-GAME
STRATEGY

The mid-game phase of a game is usually the longest. It starts after the first four or five rounds and continues until the players are near the point of becoming uninterlocked. Most of the doubling and roll-over usage occurs during the mid-game phase, and most games end during this phase with a player being doubled out. The mid-game strategy is the most difficult, and considerable experience is needed to be an effective mid-game player. In this chapter, you will learn a lot of the mid-game strategy that will give you a running start in becoming an effective player during this phase of the game. There is plenty of room to improve your mid-game ability through playing experience and studying the game.

The mid-game phase is like the middle of a tennis point where both players are volleying and trying to make a good approach shot so that they can come to the net and put the point away (like doubling the other player out).

MID-GAME MOVE STRATEGY

7-1. You should hit an opponent's blot, make a point for your blockade or else-where, bring builder(s) into position to make a point, or move a runner, in that order of priority

For every move during the mid-game phase, identify each alternative move and decide whether to hit an opponent's blot, make a point for your blockade or elsewhere, bring builder(s) into position to subse-quently make a point, or move a runner. Your preference should usu-ally be in that order of priority. If you have a man on the bar, you have to enter it first. Also, you need to decide whether to use your roll-over for each unfortunate roll for you that you or your opponent makes.

7-2. By fifth roll start giving priority to escaping with runners

You should give top priority to building a blockade. However, start giving priority to escaping with your runners by your fifth roll, particularly if your opponent has built a four-point blockade. Try to escape with at least one of your runners before your opponent has a five-point blockade, because it can be tough to get past a five-point blockade. It's impossible to get past a prime, and you'll almost certainly lose the game if you get trapped behind a prime. If your opponent has not built a four-point blockade, you do not have to worry too much

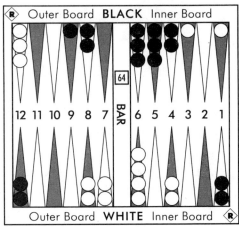

Figure 7-1

about moving your runners except to split them with a 1 or 2 roll.

You have rolled a 5-4 in Figure 7-1 for your fourth roll. Escape with the runner on your opponent's 3-point to safety on your opponent's 12-point. Then give some priority to escaping with your other runner, especially if your opponent makes his 3-, 7-, or 9-point.

7-3. Be reluctant to give up 12-point too soon; try to escape with runners first

You're more likely to escape safely with your runners if you still own your opponent's 12-point. This provides a safe landing spot for your runners. Owning the 12-point also provides a safe spot for builders to build your blockade, and a safe spot for shooters to hit opponent's blots in your outer board. For these reasons it's also important not to reduce the 12-point to two men earlier than necessary.

7-4. Do not give up your 6-point or 8-point until you are ready to start bearing off

You own your 6-point and 8-point at the beginning of the game. Only two or three of the men on your 6-point should be moved to make other inner board points. The other two or three men shouldn't be moved until you are bearing men off. Continue to own your 8-point as part of your blockade unless you roll a 1-1 or 3-3.

7-5. Usually do not hit a blot in your inner board unless you can point on it

Usually, it's better not to hit a blot in your inner board unless you can point on it because it's too dangerous to leave a shot in your inner board. If your blot is hit, you lose around 3 rolls and the hit man may become trapped.

You have rolled a 5-3 in Figure 7-2 and are 1 roll ahead. This situation is an exception. Hit the blot on your 4-point by moving the man from your 9-point to your 4-point with the 5, and move a man from your opponent's 12-point to your 10-point with the 3 for the following reasons:

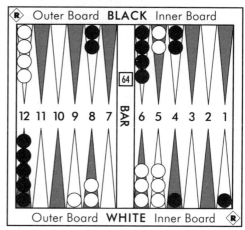

Figure 7-2

• You are at least as likely to be hit with alternate moves.
• Some of the alternate moves strip the builders from your opponent's 12-point.
• You hit a blot and put a blot on a high priority point to make.
• You have three builders to cover the blot on your 4-point.
• If you can make your 4-point, you will have a large lead.
• If your blot is hit, it isn't in trouble because your opponent doesn't have a blockade and you own his 5-point.

7-6. If you can hit two blots, you should usually do so unless they are in your inner board

If you hit two blots, you often set your opponent back 4 to 5 rolls and put two men on the bar. But if this leaves one or two shots in your inner board, it's probably too risky.

7-7. The "hit and run" can be an effective move

In the "hit and run," you hit an opponent's blot with one of your men and then move that man on to safety. This

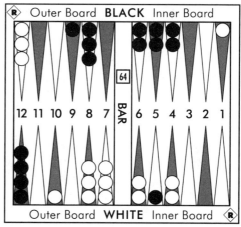

Figure 7-3

can be particularly effective in your inner board where it's too dangerous to leave a shot.

You have rolled a 2-1 in Figure 7-3. Hit the blot on your 5-point with a man from your 7-point and then move your shooter on to safety to your 4-point. There is no better way to use the 2-1 and the opponent's blot is threatening to escape. He will have to use half of his next roll to enter the man from the bar.

7-8. Usually enter a man from bar onto lowest possible point

Usually it's best to enter a man from the bar onto the lowest possible point in your opponent's inner board. You want to enter the man onto the 1-point or 2-point, unless you can hit an opponent's blot, cover your blot on a higher point, or need to escape quickly. If you enter your man onto a low point, the man is safer and has a better shot at opponent's blots in his inner board.

7-9. In at least 70% of games, you will hit at least two of opponent's men

Even if your opponent's runners escape, continue to build your blockade because it's likely that you'll hit two or more of your opponent's men. You want to have your blockade ready to trap a man or men when you hit them.

7-10. Blockade with forward gap is better than solid blockade if opponent's man is next to it

In Figure 7-4, you have a five-point blockade with a forward gap. Your opponent has to roll a 6-2 or 5-2 (11% chance) for his runner to escape. If your blockade were solid, extending from your 4-point through your 8-point, and your opponent's runner were next to it on your 3-point, the runner could escape with any 6 (31% chance). Therefore, a blockade with a forward gap is better. Needless to say, a prime is by far the best blockade to have.

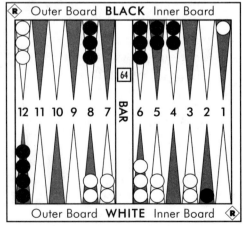

Figure 7-4

7-11. When both you and opponent are trapped behind a blockade, timing is critical because the player that has to collapse his blockade first will probably lose

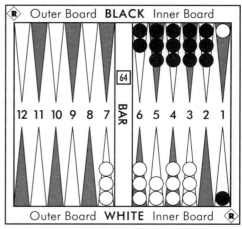

Figure 7-5

You should usually avoid hitting an opponent's blot when you need your opponent to collapse his blockade before you collapse yours. Hitting his blot will probably slow him up so he won't have to collapse his blockade until you have collapsed yours. This is an important principle because it occurs often.

You have rolled a 3-2 in Figure 7-5. You could point on the opponent's blot on your 1-point, but that would probably cause you to collapse your blockade first. Your opponent would have a man on the bar and wouldn't have to move to collapse his blockade until the man has entered. The correct play is to move a man from your 7-point and a man from your 6-point. This gives you good timing because your opponent will probably have to collapse his blockade first. If this happens, your man on the opponent's 1-point will escape easily.

If possible, move so that you can play a subsequent 5 or 6 without having to collapse your blockade. In some cases you can move so that you don't have to play a subsequent 6.

You have rolled a 6-2 in Figure 7-6. You could complete your prime by making your 2-point. This would make it likely that you would have to collapse your blockade first, particularly if you roll some 5s and 6s. It would be difficult for your man on your opponent's 1-point to escape, and your opponent would be favored to win the game. In this situation, it's more important for you to use the 6-2 roll to escape with

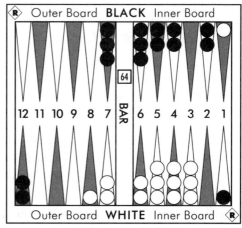

Figure 7-6

your trapped man. If this man isn't hit by the men on your 12-point, you will most likely win the game.

Double 6s and 5s are a disaster when they force you to collapse your blockade first. This allows your opponent's man or men to escape easily while your man or men are still trapped. In these timing situations, don't double unless you're fairly certain that your opponent will have to collapse his blockade first.

7-12. When behind in game, give some priority to making opponent's 4-, 5-, or 7-point

It can be effective to make your opponent's 4-, 5-, or 7-point as an anchor, particularly when you are behind in the game. The benefits of this are that it:
• Makes it easier to escape from your opponent's inner board.
• Prevents your opponent from making his 4-, 5-, or 7-point.
• Provides a safe landing spot in your opponent's board. Having an anchor in your opponent's inner board reduces your chance of being gammoned.
• Increases your chance of hitting a blot in your opponent's outer board.

It's better to make your opponent's 5-point than his 7-point. It can be effective to make your opponent's 4-point if you cannot make his 5-point or 7-point.

Don't give priority to making these points when you are ahead because you should only hold them temporarily if you aren't behind. It becomes increasingly difficult to escape safely from these points as the game progresses because your opponent will be able to quickly and safely build his inner board behind your anchor.

7-13. When more than 1 roll behind, stay back to hit rather than run

When you're significantly behind in a game, keep one or two men back in your opponent's board(s) to hit your opponent and take the lead. If you have built a strong blockade, you'll have a good chance of winning when you hit a man. If you run instead with your back man or men when significantly behind, you'll most likely lose the race and game. On the other hand, try to bring your back man or men to safety and turn the game into a race if you're ahead in the game.

You have rolled a 6-3 in Figure 7-7. You could try to escape from your opponent's 1-point with your back man. Since you are 1.5 rolls behind, though, leave your back man where it is and try to hit your opponent. Move a man from your 8-point and a man from your 6-point instead.

7-14. Leave an indirect shot, if necessary, to avoid leaving a direct shot later

You have rolled a 5-2 in Figure 7-8. You could move safely by moving a man from your opponent's 12-point to your 6-point, but that would make it likely that you would have to leave a direct shot in the next couple of turns. You need to avoid this since your opponent is building a good blockade. Instead, move a man from your opponent's 12-point to your 11-point and another man from your opponent's 12-point to your 8-point. This leaves an indirect shot on your 11-point, but it greatly increases your chance of making your 5-, 7-, or 9-point in your next turn. This, in turn, makes it much

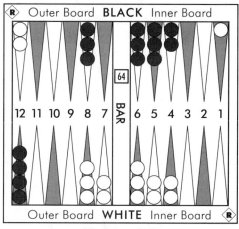

Figure 7-7

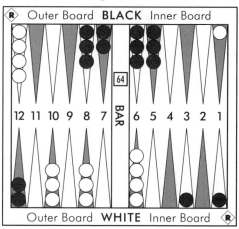

Figure 7-8

less likely that you'll have to leave a direct shot in the future.

7-15. You can be more willing to leave a shot when opponent has blot(s) in his inner board or does not have a blockade

It isn't as bad to be hit when your opponent has a blot in his inner board or doesn't have a good blockade. In fact, your opponent may decide not to hit your blot if he has a blot in his inner board. Therefore, you can be more willing to leave a shot in these situations, if necessary.

7-16. If you have to leave a direct shot, hit an opponent's man if possible

If you hit a man when you have to leave a direct shot, your opponent has to use part of his next roll to enter the man. This makes it much less likely that he will be able to hit your blot. He may even roll poorly, fail to enter, and not be able to move at all.

You have rolled a 6-5 in Figure 7-9. Move a man from your opponent's 12-point to your 7-point with the 6. For the 5, you either have to move a man from your 7-point or another man from

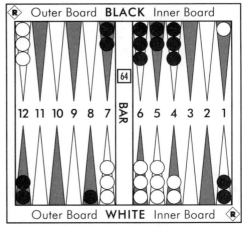

Figure 7-9

your opponent's 12-point. Both of these moves leave a direct shot. You should move a man from your opponent's 12-point because that hits the opponent's man on your 8-point. In addition to forcing your opponent to enter this man, this sends the man back and traps it.

7-17. If you have to leave a blot, try to leave it on an important point to make

When you have to leave a blot and have a choice, leave it on an important point for you to make such as your 4-, 5-, or 7-point. If you can cover your blot before it's hit, you have made an important point for your blockade. If you can, leave the blot where your opponent has the smallest chance of hitting it, on a point where he has only one shooter in range.

7-18. If you have to leave two shots, try to leave them so it takes the same number to hit them

You have a 1 left to play in Figure 7-10. Regardless of how you play the 1, you have to leave two shots. Move the man from your opponent's 9-point to his 10-point. This makes it so that your opponent has to roll a 3 to be able to hit either of your blots. This reduces your chance of being hit.

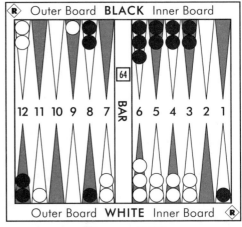

Figure 7-10

Always try to duplicate the number of a good move when you have to leave a shot. For example, if you have to leave a shot and your opponent needs to roll a 4 to make his 5-point, leave your blot four points from his shooter if you can. If your opponent rolls a 4, he may decide to make his 5-point rather than hit your blot.

7-19. Take a chance to win a gammon or backgammon if it doesn't greatly reduce chance of winning game

If you take a chance to win a gammon, you have to win at least two gammons for each game you lose as a result of taking the chance for it to be worthwhile. This principle occurs often and can significantly increase you point winnings.

You have a 2 to play in Figure 7-11. You can play safely and certainly win the game by moving the man on your 10-point to your 8-point completing your prime. However, you can and should greatly increase your chance of winning a gammon by hitting the blot on your 11-point with a man from your opponent's 12-point. This reduces your chance of winning the game some because you leave some blots and do not complete your prime. Since this doesn't greatly reduce your chance of winning the game, it's worth increasing your chance of winning a gammon.

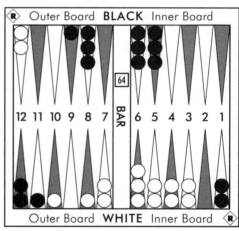

Figure 7-11

You have rolled a 5-2 in Figure 7-12. You have to enter your man from the bar with the 2. You could play safely by moving the entered man onto your opponent's 7-point. But playing aggressively for a gammon by hitting the man on your 1-point

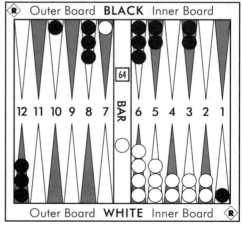

Figure 7-12

with the 5 is better. If you can then cover your man on your 1-point before your opponent enters, you will almost certainly win a gammon. You're much more likely to cover your man than your opponent is to enter hitting your man.

PROBABILITIES

The following principles give you the chances of entering men, making a point, and rolling a particular number or combination of numbers. The tables are formed using Table 3-1. If you cannot remember all of the numbers, at least have a good feel for the chance of entering men, making points, and rolling specific numbers. This is important in making your move, doubling, and roll-over decisions.

Making the best move or decision according to the probabilities won't pay off every time. It won't allow you to win every game and every set. Using the best strategy according to the probabilities, though, will pay off in the long run and allow you to win more matches than you would otherwise.

7-20. Chance of entering one man from bar is shown in Table 7-1

While you don't want to have a man hit, Table 7-1 shows that the man usually has a good chance of entering. Even if only two points are open (four points covered or owned by your opponent) in your

Table 7-1

Number of points covered	Rolls that enter	Chance of entering one man
1	35	97%
2	32	89%
3	27	75%
4	20	56%
5	11	31%

opponent's inner board, you have more than a 50% chance of entering a man. If your opponent only has two of his inner board points covered, you have an 89% chance of entering. Obviously, you have a 0% chance of entering if your opponent has all six of his inner board points covered.

7-21. Chance of entering two men from bar with one roll is shown in Table 7-2

If you have two men on the bar, your chance of entering both of them with one roll is fairly low, as shown in Table 7-2. There is an easy way to remember the numbers in this table.

Table 7-2

Number of points covered	Rolls that enter	Chance of entering two men
1	25	69%
2	16	44%
3	9	25%
4	4	11%
5	1	3%

The number of rolls that enter both men is equal to the square of the number of points open. For example, if there are four points open (your opponent has two points covered in his inner board), there are 4 × 4 = 16 rolls that enter. You can easily see that the chance of entering both men in this case is a little less than 50%, since, $^{16}/_{36}$ = 0.44 = 44%.

7-22. Chance of making a point is shown in Table 7-3

Table 7-3 shows that you need a large number of builders within six points of the point you are trying to make to have a high probability of making the point.

In Figure 7-13, you have four builders to make your 3-point. Thus, you have a 39% chance of making your 3-point and completing your prime in the next roll. Your opponent has two builders (7% chance) for making his 7-point and completing his prime in the next roll.

Table 7-3

Number of builders	Chance of making point
2	7%
3	19%
4	39%
5	61%
6	92%

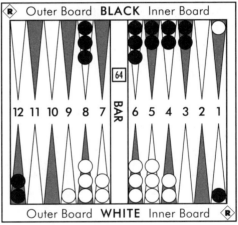

Figure 7-13

7-23. Chance of rolling a specific number is shown in Table 7-4

The chance of rolling a specific number, such as a 6 or a 1, is shown in Table 7-4. For example, if you need to roll a 6 for your runner to escape, you have a 31% chance of escaping in one roll and a 52% chance of escaping in two rolls.

Table 7-4

Number of rolls	Chance of rolling number
1	31%
2	52%
3	67%

7-24. Chance of rolling a 5 or 6 is shown in Table 7-5

The chance of rolling a 5 or 6 is shown in Table 7-5. If you need to roll either a 5 or a 6 for your runner to escape, you have a 56% chance of escaping in one roll and an 80% chance of escaping in two rolls. This table applies for rolling one of any two numbers, such as a 2 or a 4. Thus, you can also use this table when you have a man on the bar and your opponent owns four of the points in his inner board (two points open) to determine your chance of entering in one, two, or three rolls.

7-25. Chance of rolling a specific combination such as 6-1 is shown in Table 7-6

Table 7-6 shows that your chance of escaping is small if you have a man trapped behind a five-point blockade and the man isn't next to the blockade. For example, your chance of escaping is only 16% even with three rolls if you need to roll a 6-1 to escape. Table 7-4 shows that your chance of escaping is much larger if you move the trapped man to be adjacent to the blockade.

You have rolled a 4-2 in Figure 7-14. You might be tempted to move your runner on your opponent's 1-point to his 3-point with the 2 to be closer to the blockade. Instead, you should move the blot on your 10-point to your 4-point. You want to move your runner to your opponent's 4-point to be next to the blockade. Table 3-2 shows that you have a larger chance of getting your runner to your opponent's 4-point if it's on his 1-point rather than on his 3-point.

Table 7-5

Number of rolls	Chance of 5 or 6
1	56%
2	80%
3	91%

Table 7-6

Number of rolls	Chance of combo
1	6%
2	11%
3	16%

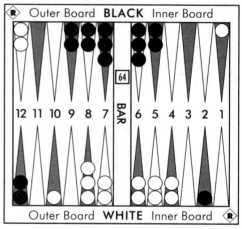

Figure 7-14

MID-GAME DOUBLING STRATEGY

I will now show you several mid-game phase doubling principles or situations using the doubling principles that you learned in Chapter 4. It's white's turn in each of these situations. This should give you a better feel for the chance of winning the game in various mid-game situations, and whether to double or accept a double. You need to update your doubling assessment each turn before you roll to decide whether to double.

7-26. In Figures 7-15 and 7-16, white has 66% chance of winning and can consider doubling

White has a 66% chance of winning the game in Figures 7-15 and 7-16, which is more than the minimum required to consider doubling (63%). White should wait at least one round to achieve a larger lead before doubling in these mid-game situations. However, white should double now if he is considerably behind in the set. Black should accept in both of these situations if white doubles.

7-27. In Figures 7-17 and 7-18, white has 70% chance of winning and should double; black should accept

In Figures 7-17 and 7-18, white has a 70% chance of winning the game. White has a lead that is just large enough to double and should double. Black should accept.

7-28. In Figure 7-19 white has 74% chance of winning and should double; black should accept

In Figure 7-19, white has near the optimum lead for doubling and should definitely double. Black should accept because he has more than a 25% chance of winning the game.

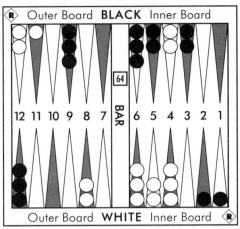
Figure 7-15

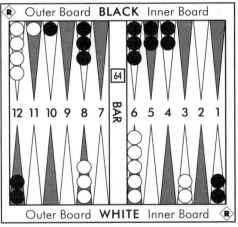
Figure 7-16

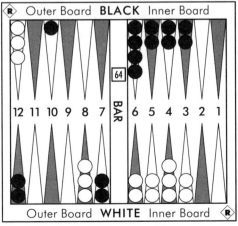
Figure 7-17

7-29. In Figure 7-20 white has 76% chance of winning and should double; black should resign

In Figure 7-20, white should definitely double and black should resign. Black has less than a 25% chance of winning the game.

7-30. In Figure 7-21 white has 83% chance of winning and should wait to double

In Figure 7-21, white's lead is too large to double. White should wait at least one round to double because black would certainly decline a double and white is unlikely to lose much of his lead in the next round. Also, white has a decent chance of winning a gammon.

When you first look at the situation shown on the title page of this book, you might conclude that black has a huge lead and will certainly win the game. Actually, white, who owns the doubling cube, should double and black should resign because white has about a 76% chance of winning the game. White still has his roll-over and black has used his, so white has two chances to roll a 4 or a 6 to hit black's blot. Table 7-5 shows that white has an 80% chance of doing this. If white hits the blot, then black is trapped

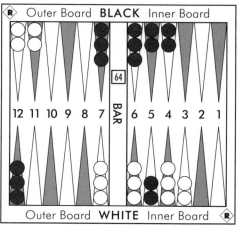

Figure 7-18

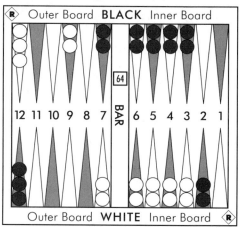

Figure 7-19

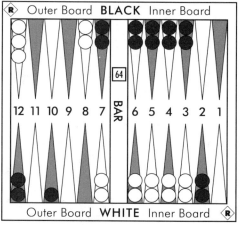

Figure 7-20

76

behind white's prime and white has about a 95% chance of winning the game (Principle 3-13). If white doesn't hit the blot, he will certainly lose. Therefore, white has around $0.8 \times 0.95 = 0.76 = 76\%$ chance of winning the game and should double in the title page situation. This is another of the countless reasons why I find backgammon to be such an intriguing, fascinating game.

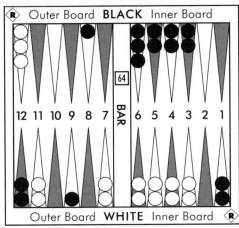

Figure 7-21

8. END-GAME STRATEGY

The end-game phase of a game starts when the players are near the point of becoming uninterlocked and continues until they start to bear men off. In this phase the game changes into a race, but there is still a good chance that men will be hit.

The end-game and bearing off phases are similar to when a golfer gets on the green. He needs to make a good approach putt to make sure he takes no more than two putts total to hole out (like bearing off first).

END-GAME MOVE STRATEGY

8-1. Timing can be critical when both players have to break an outer board point to bring the men to safety

It's your opponent's turn in Figure 8-1 and you are nearly even in the race. It will take both of you about three rolls to get all of your men into your inner boards if you can get past each other quickly and safely. You have better timing than your opponent because he will have to break the point that is in your outer board and leave a shot if he rolls a 6-1, 6-2, 6-3, 6-4, or 6-5. Hang tight on your opponent's 11-point until you can move those men safely or hit your opponent. You can still play a couple of 6s without having to move those men. It's important to try to move so that your opponent has to break his outer board point first in common situations like this. If possible, move so

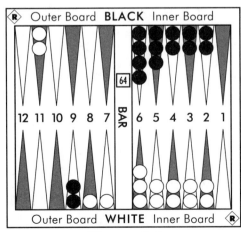

Figure 8-1

that you can play a subsequent 5 or 6 without having to break your outer board point first.

8-2. When you are nearly uninterlocked and ahead, carefully try to turn the game into a straight race

You have rolled a 5-2 in Figure 8-2. You are ahead, by about half a roll, so try to turn the game into a straight race by moving the men from your opponent's 10-point. You can then, most likely, move the men safely from your opponent's 12-point, win the race, and win the game. On the other hand, if you're behind in a situation like this, stay interlocked trying to hit your opponent to gain the lead.

8-3. When you are one or more rolls behind, hit a man even if you have to leave a shot

You have rolled a 2-1 and are one roll behind in Figure 8-3. Hit the blot with a man from your 8-point even though this will leave a direct shot in your inner board. If you don't hit the blot, it will most likely escape and your opponent would have a high chance (about 75%) of winning the game. If you hit the blot, you will gain a roll or more and increase your chance of winning the game to around 50% or more. Your opponent will have a 56% chance of entering and only a 31% chance of hitting your blot.

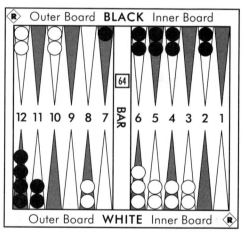

Figure 8-2

8-4. In a straight race, get all of your men to your outer board before you move more men to your inner board

In a straight race (players no longer interlocked), the most

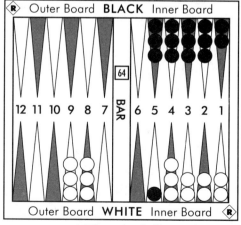

Figure 8-3

efficient way to get your men into your inner board is to get them all into your outer board before moving any men that are in your outer board. Similarly, get all of your men into your inner board before moving any men that are in your inner board.

8-5. In a straight race, get all your men into your inner board as quickly as possible, even if it means stacking men on your 6-point

Since you cannot start bearing men off until you have all of your men in your inner board, get your men into your inner board as quickly as possible in a straight race, even if it means stacking men on your 6-point. This also makes maximum use of double 6s and 5s and 6-5s after you get all of your men into your inner board. Although an even distribution is desirable, it's not as important in a straight race. But if you can get your men in evenly without sacrificing speed, do it.

Use the same strategy in getting your men into your inner board as you use for bearing men off, both when you are interlocked and in a straight race. You will learn this strategy in the next chapter.

You have rolled a 6-3 in Figure 8-4. Since you cannot bring both of the men in your outer board into your inner board, move the man on your 10-point to your vacant 4-point. Then move the man on your 11-point to your 8-point. You will be able to bear at least one man off in your next turn, which is the best you can do.

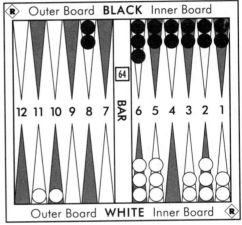

Figure 8-4

END-GAME DOUBLING STRATEGY

8-6. Pip count is about 54 when all men are in inner board evenly distributed

When all of your men are in your inner board evenly distributed, your pip count is about 54. This means that your men have to move a total of about 54 points in this situation to be all borne off.

When you bring your last man into your inner board, your pip count is usually about 65 since there will probably be many more men on your 4-, 5-, and 6-points than on your 1-, 2-, and 3-points. This and the preceding principle are important ones to use in conjunction with Principle 4-8 to determine whether to double or accept a double during a straight race and when the game will likely become a straight race.

It's your turn in Figure 8-5. Using Principle 3-20, you can quickly see that you are 1 roll ahead (6 − 5), so try to become uninterlocked to make the game a straight race. Also, double because you are about (5% + 3) pips ahead and your inner board distribution is equal to your opponent's (Principle 4-8). You determine this using the following simple calculation. You are 5 rolls or around 40 pips (5 × 8) from having all of your men into your inner board. Therefore, your pip count is about (40 + 65) or about 105, and 5% of 105 is 5.25, so (5% + 3) = (5.25 + 3) = 8.25 pips. You are 1 roll or around 8 pips ahead, which is about (5% + 3) or about 8.25 pips ahead.

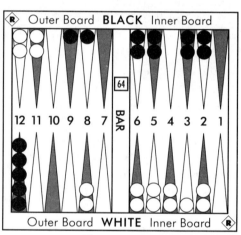

Figure 8-5

Your opponent should accept because you have approximately a 74% chance of winning.

9. Bearing Off

Bearing off is the last phase of a game, and it starts when a player has all of his men in his inner board. If the players are no longer interlocked, the game is now a race to bear men off quickly and efficiently. If the players are still interlocked, safety is top priority in bearing off. Many games are won or lost during this phase of the game when a player surges from behind to win.

BEARING OFF WHEN INTERLOCKED

Although your opponent has a prime in the following situations, make the recommended moves regardless of whether your opponent has a prime or not. When your opponent has a prime, it's extremely important that you make the correct moves.

You also need to be careful when your opponent has a speed board. He has a speed board when all of his men are on his 1-, 2-, and 3-points except for the man (or men) that you have trapped. Since he will bear his men off quickly when he escapes, you probably need to bear at least a few men off before he gets away and you need to avoid being hit.

9-1. When bearing off with opponent in your inner board or on bar, vacate the highest point first rather than creating open points between your men

When bearing off while interlocked, vacate your 6-point first, then vacate your 5-point, etc. If you create an open point between your men when bearing off, you're more likely to have to leave a shot.

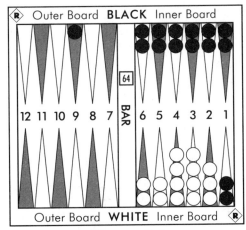

Figure 9-1

You will see in the next principle, though, that you should avoid leaving three men on your highest point.

In Figure 9-1, you have rolled a 3-3. Move the two men on both your 6-point and 5-point instead of bearing off the four men on your 3-point.

9-2. When bearing off with opponent in your inner board or on bar, avoid leaving odd number of men on highest two points. Avoid leaving three men on highest point if it is less than 6-point

If you have an odd number of men on your highest points, you are likely to have to leave a blot. Large rolls like 6-6, 5-5, and 6-5 will leave a blot and can be disastrous.

In Figure 9-2, you have rolled a 6-2. You have to bear a man off from your 6-point with the 6. The most efficient move for the 2 would be to bear a man off from your 2-point. But that would leave an odd number of total men on your 5-point and 6-point. Move a man from your 5-point to your 3-point with the 2 to keep an even number of men on both your highest and your highest two points. In this situation, you'll win the game easily if you aren't hit.

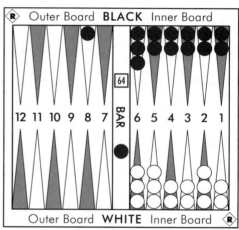

Figure 9-2

You'll lose the game if you are hit by the man on the bar in the next few rolls. You must make safe moves even if they aren't efficient.

9-3. When bearing off with opponent in your inner board or on bar, remember that you are not required to bear a man off if there is an alternate legal move

In Figure 9-3, you have rolled a 6-3. You have to bear a man off from your 5-point with the 6. You could bear a man off from your 3-point with the 3 to be most efficient, but that would leave a shot on your 5-point. Instead, use the 3 to move the man from your 5-point to your 2-point to avoid leaving a shot.

If you roll a 4-3 instead in Figure 9-3, you could bear two men off, from your 3-point and 4-point. This would leave an odd number of men on your highest two points, which is unsafe. In this situation, move your men from your 5-point to your 1-point and 2-point to be safe instead of bearing men off.

9-4. Remember that you can play the dice in either order

In Figure 9-4, you had to leave a shot on your previous roll, but your opponent didn't hit you. If you now roll a 6-1, play the 1 first by moving the man from your 6-point to your 5-point. Then you use the 6 to bear the man off from your 5-point. This doesn't leave a shot. It doesn't make maximum use of the roll, but you don't have to make maximum use of the roll since you used both dice. If you play the 6 first to bear the man off from your 6-point, then you would have to leave a shot with the 1.

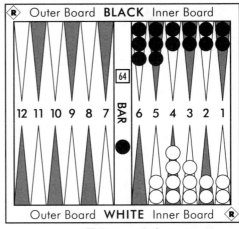

Figure 9-3

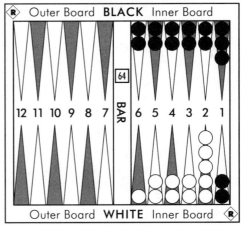

Figure 9-4

If you roll a 6-4 in Figure 9-4, you could use the 4 first by moving the man from your 6-point to your 2-point, then bear a man off from your 5-point with the 6. The other way to play this roll is to bear off the man from your 6-point and bear a man off from your 4-point. Both alternatives leave a shot, but the second alternative is better since it bears two men off.

BEARING OFF WHEN NOT INTERLOCKED

9-5. When bearing off and not interlocked, always bear a man off in preference to moving a man within the inner board

In Figure 9-5, you have rolled a 3-2. You may be tempted to move two men forward, from your 5-point and 6-point to achieve a more uniform distribution. When you're no longer interlocked, though, it's much more important to bear men off than to maintain a uniform distribution. Always bear two (or more) men off when you can. So bear the men off from your 2-point and 3-point.

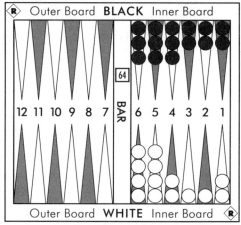

Figure 9-5

9-6. For bearing off, add ¼ roll for each extra empty low point and each extra man on high points

In Figure 9-6, you have three more men on your 4-point through 6-point than your opponent and one more empty low point, so you are around ⁴⁄₄ or 1 roll (8 pips) behind. You learned earlier to resign a double if you are (5% + 3) or more pips behind in a straight race. A player's pip count is about 54 when all of his men are in his inner board evenly distributed. Therefore, your opponent's pip count is about 54 in Figure 9-6, and (5% + 3) of 54 is around (3 + 3) or 6. Since you are about 8 pips behind, which is more than 6, your opponent should double if it's his turn and you should resign.

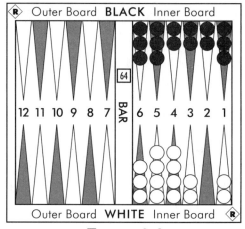

Figure 9-6

Use this principle in combination with Principle 3-20 to accurately estimate the number of rolls that you are ahead or behind at any point in the game.

9-7. When there are only a few rolls left in the game, double if your opponent needs at least as many rolls as you to bear off

When there are six or fewer rolls left for you to bear the rest of your men off, count the number of rolls required for you and your opponent to bear your remaining men off. Account for differences in distribution using the previous principle and double if your opponent needs at least as many rolls as you to bear off. Decline your opponent's double if you need at least 0.5 roll more than him to bear off. You should also decline if you need at least as many rolls to bear off with just one or two rolls left.

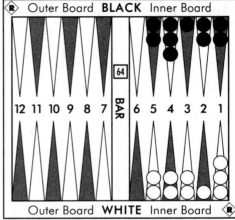

Figure 9-7

With only a few rolls left in a game, giving the doubling cube to your opponent isn't nearly as significant as it is earlier in the game. Late in the game it's not likely that your opponent will gain enough ground to double you out, so you can double late in the game with only a small lead.

It's your turn in Figure 9-7 and the right thing to do is double. Both you and your opponent should need 5 rolls to bear the rest of your men off. Since it's your turn, you're significantly more likely to win. Your opponent should accept your double.

9-8. Double with more than a 50% chance of winning when only one roll is left in game

When there is only one roll left in a game, giving the doubling cube up by doubling has no significance. Thus, you don't need a 63% chance of winning to consider doubling in this case. Double if you have more than a 50% chance of winning. You'll win more points in the long run by doing this.

9-9. Chance of bearing one or two men off with one roll is shown in Table 9-1

When you have only one or two men left to bear off, you can determine the chance of bearing both

Table 9-1

Points man/men are on	Rolls that bear off	Chance of bearing both off
6 & 4	8	22%
6 & 3	10	28%
6 & 1	15	42%
4 & 3	17	47%
5 & 2	19	53%
3 & 2	25	69%
2 & 2	26	72%
6	27	75%
4 & 1	29	81%
5	31	86%
4	34	94%

of them off with the next roll from Table 9-1. Use this, in combination with your opponent's chance of bearing all of his men off, to determine whether to double or accept a double. Table 9-1 shows, for example, that you should double if your last two men are on your 5-point and 2-point (or closer) and your opponent will certainly bear the rest of his men off in his next roll, since this is the last roll of the game and you have a 53% chance of winning. Resign your opponent's double if he will certainly bear the rest of his men off in two rolls and your last two men are on your 6-point and 4-point (or higher).

It's your turn in Figure 9-8, you own the cube, and you have a 53% chance of bearing your two men off. In this case, don't double, because your opponent has an 86% chance of bearing his man off (see Table 9-1), rather than 100%. If you double, then you must bear your men off or your opponent will double you out. If you don't double and don't bear both men off, you still have a 14% chance of winning (100 − 86) because you still own the cube and your opponent cannot double you out.

9-10. Chance of bearing two men off in two rolls is shown in Table 9-2

When you have two men left on your high points, use Table 9-2 to determine your chance

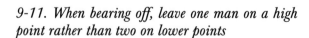

Figure 9-8

of bearing both of them off in two rolls. Then use this information in your doubling strategy near the end of a game. For example, this shows that you should always double when you have two or fewer men left and your opponent will certainly require two rolls to bear his men off.

Table 9-2

Points men are on	Chance of bearing both off
6 & 6	78%
6 & 5	88%
6 & 4	93%
6 & 3	97%

9-11. When bearing off, leave one man on a high point rather than two on lower points

You're more likely to bear a man off from a high point than two men from lower points (unless they are on the 1-point and either the 2-point or 3-point). This can be seen from Table 9-1. Thus, bear a man off leaving a man on a high point if necessary, rather than move a man forward in your inner board to leave two men on lower points.

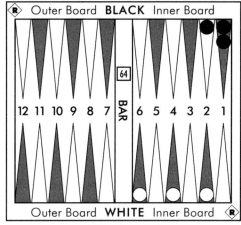

You have rolled a 4-2 in Figure 9-9. Bear the men off from the 4-point and 2-point instead of bearing off the man from the 6-point. This gives you a 75% chance of bearing the man off from the 6-point next

Figure 9-9

turn. If you bear off the man from the 6-point, you will have only a 64% chance of bearing the men off from the 4-point and 2-point next turn.

Table 9-1 also shows that it's better for you to have your men on the 5-point and 2-point than on the 4-point and 3-point. It's also better to have your men on the 4-point and 1-point than on the 3-point and 2-point.

It's better to have two men split on two points than to have them on the same point. For example, it's better to have your last two men on the 3-point and 1-point than to have them both on the 2-point.

9-12. When you have to bear the rest of your men off next turn, maximize your chance of doing so

In Figure 9-10, you have rolled a 1-1. Your opponent will bear the rest of his men off with two rolls, so you will have only one more roll. Your only logical move is to bear the men off from your 1-point and use the other two 1s to move the men from your 3-point to your 2-point. Although your chance of winning isn't good, this makes it so that you need double 2s or better, rather than double 3s or better, to bear your remaining men off.

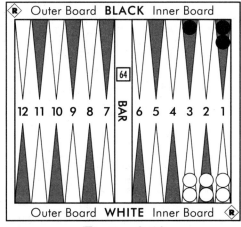

Figure 9-10

10. THE BACK GAME

A back game can be exciting because the lead can change hands quickly and substantially. This type of game occurs when a player is considerably behind, owns most or all of his inner board points, owns one or two of the opponent's inner board points, and is hoping to hit a man as the opponent is bearing men off. If the back game player hits a man, he can often trap that man long enough to take the lead and win the game. With the back game, he has a reasonable chance of changing his fortune from being desperately behind to winning the game. The problem is that a back game is not successful often enough and the back game player is frequently gammoned or even backgammoned. So avoid getting into a back game situation. However, you need to know the correct back game doubling strategy and how to conduct an effective back game because there are occasions when this type of game is necessary. Also, you need to know how to play against a back game because your opponent will occasionally conduct one.

The back game reminds me of an ice hockey team playing short-handed against the other team's power play. They are trying desperately to keep the other team from scoring (bearing completely off) and to score short-handed (hit opponent).

BACK GAME DOUBLING STRATEGY

10-1. Double opponent back game if chance of winning gammon is not good (less than 40%)

Although a back game is exciting, it's a losing proposition. Double your opponent if he is in a back game situation unless you have a good chance (greater than 40%) of winning a gammon. Actually, you probably should have doubled before he started conducting the back game. If you have a good chance of winning a gammon, continue to try for the gammon. If it becomes too risky to continue or your chance for a gammon decreases, double.

In Figure 10-1 your opponent has a good back game position. Because you have about a 65% chance of winning the game and a decent, but not good, chance of winning a gammon, double. Your opponent's back game position is too good for you to continue to try for a gammon. He must pay for the chance to have his back game work by accepting your double.

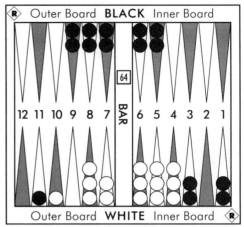

Figure 10-1

10-2. Decline double when in back game

Nearly always decline a double when you are in a back game situation unless your opponent would win the set with your resignation. Your chance of winning the game is usually too small (less than 30%) and your chance of losing a gammon or backgammon is too large to accept a double in a back game situation. In fact, you'll usually be thankful for a double and a way out of the back game situation to avoid losing a gammon.

If your back game is well-timed with two good points in your opponent's inner board, you can accept a double. You will probably lose fewer points by accepting the double and playing an all-out back game in these cases.

CONDUCTING A BACK GAME

While you should avoid getting into a back game situation, there will be occasions when you need to conduct a good back game. When you're desperately behind in a game and your opponent doesn't double, you'll need to play a good back game to have a chance of winning the game and avoiding a gammon. There are several reasons or situations why your opponent may not double when you are in a back game situation:

• He doesn't know that he should double you.

• His chance of winning the game is too high (more than 80%) to double.

• He is playing for a gammon.

• You own the doubling cube.

- The Crawford Rule is in effect so he cannot double.
- He is one point from winning the set so he shouldn't double.

10-3. The 1-point and 3-point are best for back game; next best are 2-point and 3-point

To conduct an ideal back game, you need to own two points in your opponent's inner board, as shown in Figure 10-2. The best are the 1-point and 3-point, and the next best are the 2-point and 3-point. Don't keep more than four men in your opponent's inner board because you have to have enough men to build a strong blockade to trap a man when you hit it, and so that you are less likely to be gammoned or backgammoned.

10-4. When playing a back game, try to time it so that you have a full inner board when you hit opponent

In addition to being desperately behind and owning two points in your opponent's inner board, you need to have a strong blockade in or near your inner board to conduct a good back game. Your timing needs to be good, as shown in Figure 10-2, so that you have a strong blockade or full inner

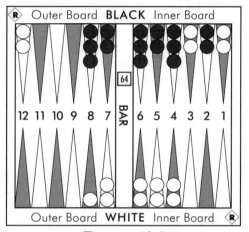

Figure 10-2

board when you hit an opponent's man. In Figure 10-2, if you get a shot at an opponent's blot, you'll probably get it within about three or four rounds. By that time there is a good chance you will own nearly all of your inner board points. If you hit a man at that time, you will have a decent chance of trapping the man and winning the game. After you hit a man, start running with your back men, do everything you can to keep the man that you hit trapped, and possibly hit other men. Keep your back men spread out as you bring them around to increase your chance of hitting the man you trapped should he escape, and to hit other men. Complete a prime as quickly as possible.

Your back game has been successful in Figure 10-3. Your timing has been good, you have hit a man, and you have started running with your back men. Continue to run with your back men and bring them to your inner board one at a time to make your 1-point quickly, and possibly hit more of his men in his inner board.

10-5. To obtain the proper timing in a back game, you may have to leave blots to entice your opponent to hit them to slow you down

Your timing is bad in Figure 10-4 because your blockade will collapse onto your 1-, 2-, and 3-point by the time you hit a man. If you hit a man, that man will enter and escape easily. You must avoid having to collapse your blockade by having one or more of your men hit to slow your progress, or by running with one or more of your back men (or both).

10-6. In a back game don't wait too long to start running with your back men

Once you have all of your men (except your back men) in your inner board, start running with your back men to avoid collapsing your blockade and to avoid a gammon.

You have rolled a 5-2 in Figure 10-5. Run with a man that is on your opponent's 3-point and make your 2-point as soon as you can. When that man is close to or in your inner board, run with the other man on your opponent's 3-point.

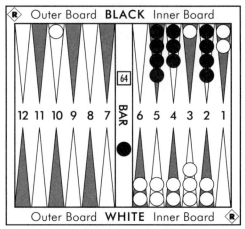

Figure 10-3

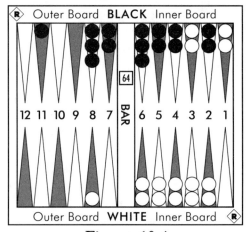

Figure 10-4

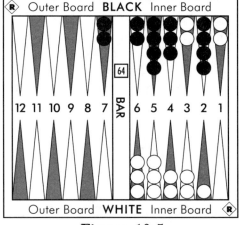

Figure 10-5

Actually, breaking your opponent's 3-point at this time doesn't substantially hurt your back game. After you run with the 5-2 roll in Figure 10-5, your opponent will have to leave a shot if he rolls a 6-5, 6-4, 5-4, or 4-3. You will have two shooters, from your opponent's 1-point and either the 3-point or bar, to hit any blots your opponent leaves.

If your back game is well-timed with two good points in your opponent's inner board, keep your back men back as long as possible (avoiding a backgammon) to hit one or more of your opponent's men. Even though you'll be gammoned sometimes, you'll lose fewer points by staying back as long as possible. You need to avoid being backgammoned, though.

It's your opponent's turn in Figure 10-6, and you have a strong back game that is well-timed. Continue to build a good blockade and caterpillar it into your inner board. Keep your back men in place as long as possible, and most likely you'll hit at least one of your opponent's men.

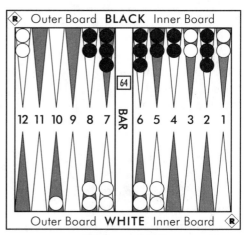

Figure 10-6

10-7. When you must hit a man, maximize your chance of hitting even if you have to leave a shot

You have a 1 to play in Figure 10-7. Move a man from your opponent's 3-point to 4-point. This maximizes your chance of hitting your opponent if he has to leave a shot. If you don't hit your opponent, you'll certainly be gammoned. If you hit your opponent, you have a good chance of winning the game. While this principle is applicable during back games, it can also apply in most game phases and situations.

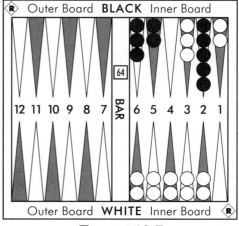

Figure 10-7

95

PLAYING AGAINST A BACK GAME

If you cannot double, your opponent accepts your double, or you are trying for a gammon when he is in a back game situation, you will have to successfully play against his back game. Don't double if you only need one point to win the set. (You can't double if your opponent owns the cube or if the Crawford Rule is in effect.)

10-8. When playing against a back game, top priority is to move safely

When your opponent is conducting a back game, you have a large lead in the game. If you aren't hit, you'll win the game and possibly a gammon or backgammon. Your top priority in this situation is to move safely. Make safe moves even if they aren't efficient moves since you can afford to lose some of your lead to avoid being hit. Use the same move strategy that you learned in the previous chapter for bearing off when interlocked.

In Figure 10-8, you have rolled a 6-3. You have to, and want to, bear a man off from your 6-point with the 6. The efficient move for the 3 would be to bear a man off from your 3-point. This would

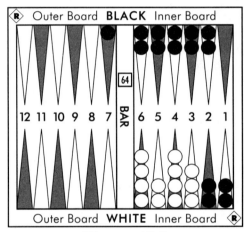

Figure 10-8

leave an uneven number of men on your highest two points, which isn't safe. Instead of bearing a man off from your 3-point, move a man from your 6-point to your 3-point with the 3. This is a safer move since it leaves two men on both your 5-point and 6-point.

10-9. When playing against a back game, move so a 5 or 6 can be safely played on next roll

Often, 5 and 6 rolls can be disastrous when you are playing against a back game or with opponent's men in your inner board. You need to try to move so 5 and 6 rolls can always be played safely.

In Figure 10-9, you have rolled a 3-1. If you don't move the men from your 8-point, a 5 or 6 (or both) on your next roll would leave one or two blots on your 7-point and 8-point. Therefore, move the men from your 8-point to your 7-point and 5-point. This makes all 5 and 6 rolls on your next roll safe since you cannot play a 6 or double 6s and you will have a third man on your 7-point to play a 5 or double 5s safely.

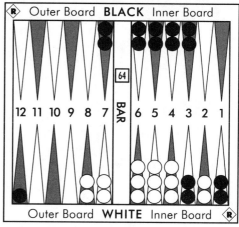

Figure 10-9

11. MATCH AND TOURNAMENT STRATEGY

Backgammon is most rewarding if you can participate in a club and tournaments. Even an informal tournament with only four players can be gratifying. Other alternatives are to get a good computer backgammon game or play on the Internet. In any case, backgammon should be played in sets and matches even if the match is only one set and the set is only five points. Know the correct set, match, and tournament strategy, and how to conduct a tournament. Some of this strategy doesn't apply if the game is played for a given amount of money for each point.

SET AND MATCH STRATEGY

11-1. When you lose a game, minimize your loss to one or two points by using correct doubling strategy, avoiding a gammon, and rarely (if ever) losing a backgammon

In Figure 11-1, you have rolled a 5-4, you have already used your rollover, and your opponent has borne nine men off. You have missed the blot and have certainly lost the game. Run with your man on the opponent's 1-point by moving it to your opponent's 10-point to avoid a gammon and possible backgammon. You'll probably need two more rolls to bear a man off, and your opponent will probably need three rolls to bear the rest of his men off. It's too risky (and foolish) not to run.

Be particularly careful to avoid a gammon if a gammon

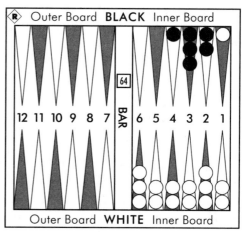

Figure 11-1

will win the set for your opponent. In this situation, avoid any moves that will risk losing a gammon.

11-2. When near end of set, use doubling strategy shown in Table 11-1

Table 11-1 shows how to modify your doubling strategy when you or your opponent is one or two points from winning the set. This table assumes that the Crawford Rule game has been played so the doubling cube can be used again when you or your oppo-

Table 11-1

Points from set		Double	Accept
You	Opp.		
1	2	Do not double	>50% game
1	3	Do not double	>40% game
2	1	Immediately	N/A
2	2	>55% game	>25% game
2	3	>75% game	>30% game
2	4	>75% game	>30% game
3	1	>55% game	N/A
3	2	>65% game	>25% game
4	1	>55% game	N/A
4	2	>60% game	>20% game

nent is one point from winning the set. Never double when you need just one point to win the set since winning the game will win the set.

When your opponent is one point and you are two points from winning the set, double immediately (before your first roll). Your opponent will probably accept so the winner of the game will win the set. This increases your chance of winning the set to 50%. If you don't double, you'll need to win two games in a row to win the set, which is only a 25% chance.

When both you and your opponent are two points from winning the set, double as soon as you're clearly ahead; that is, when you have more than a 55% chance of winning the game (>55% game). In this case, there is no consequence in giving up the cube since a subsequent double by your opponent is meaningless. Thus, you don't need to wait until you have a 63% chance of winning the game to consider doubling. Go ahead and take the greater than 55% chance of winning the set. If your opponent resigns, your chance of winning the set increases to 75% due to the Crawford Rule. If your opponent doubles instead, accept if you have more than a 25% chance of winning the game. If you resign, you'll need to win the next two games (due to the Crawford Rule) to win the set, which gives you only a 25% chance of winning the set. Thus, 25% is the break-even point for accepting a double in this situation.

When you are two points from winning the set and your opponent is three or more points from winning the set, you need a larger lead than normal to double. You should have more than a 75% chance of winning the game as shown in Table 11-1. In this case, your opponent will redouble immediately (if he accepts your double) since he must win the game or lose the set and has nothing to lose by redoubling. If he is three or four points from winning the set, he will win the set by redoubling and winning the game. If he is more than four points from winning the set, he will redouble to maximize his winnings.

When your opponent is one point and you are three or more points from winning the set, double as soon as you're clearly ahead. There is a good chance that your opponent will resign turning your 55% to 60% game instantly into a 100% game. If you doubled immediately (before your first roll), your opponent would surely accept and you would be faced with having to improve your chance of winning from 50% or less to 100% to win the game and keep the set alive.

You can use reasoning similar to the situations above to understand the strategy for the other situations shown in Table 11-1. For example, if your opponent doubles when he is two points and you are one point from winning the set and you're ahead in the game, accept the double. This gives you more than a 50% chance of winning the set. Resigning would give you only a 50% chance of winning the set since you would start a new game that you would have to win (both you and your opponent would be one point from winning the set). If you're behind in the game, resign. Resigning improves your chance to 50% of winning the set because it starts the last game of the set.

The current value of the doubling cube must be taken into account in using this strategy principle. For example, double as soon as you obtain a slight lead when you own the cube at a value of two, your opponent is one or two points from winning the set, and you are three or four points from winning the set.

11-3. When you are ahead in a set, you need a larger chance of winning than normal to double or accept a double; when you are behind in a set, double and accept a double with a smaller chance of winning than normal

When you and your opponent have the same number of points in a set, you both have a 50% chance of winning the set. If a player has more points than his opponent, he has more than a 50% chance of winning the set. Conversely, if a player has fewer points than his opponent, he has less than a 50% chance of winning the set. When you're ahead in a set, you should be conservative and have a larger chance of winning the game than normal to double or accept a double. When you're behind in a set, be more daring and double and accept a double with a smaller chance of winning the game than normal. If you are two or more points ahead or behind in a set, your doubling and acceptance points should be adjusted by 5%, 10%, or more. Some of this principle can be seen in Table 11-1.

11-4. Be more reluctant than normal to do something if it could take your opponent to the Crawford Rule game

Be more reluctant than normal in making an aggressive move, doubling, accepting a double, or declining a double if losing the game would take your opponent to the Crawford Rule game; that is, to one point from winning the set. If your opponent gets to one point from winning the set, you have less than a 25% chance of winning the set because you would need to win at least two games in a row to win the set due to the Crawford Rule.

For example, consider the case when your opponent has four points and you have two points in a seven-point set. Since you are two points behind, you should normally double when you obtain around a 65% chance of winning the game. In this case, however, wait until you have at least a 70% chance of winning the game to double since doubling and losing would take your opponent to the Crawford Rule game.

11-5. When opponent will win set if he wins game, go all out to win game even at risk of being gammoned or backgammoned

If your opponent will win the set by winning the game, double (if your opponent doesn't own the cube) and go all out to win the game. You can even risk losing a gammon or backgammon if necessary. Since you'll lose the set by losing the game, it doesn't matter how many points you lose.

11-6. On average, six to seven games are played in a seven-point set

An average of about 1.8 points are won each game due to doubles and occasional gammons and backgammons. An average of around 11 points are won each set, usually seven by the set winner and about four by the other player. Therefore, there is an average of six to seven games ($^{11}/_{1.8}$) in a set. You usually have to win four games to win the set, and you can usually lose three games and still win the set. If you lose a couple games, don't panic.

TOURNAMENT STRATEGY

Now that you have learned the correct strategy for playing games, sets, and matches, you're ready to play and win. If you haven't done so already, find someone to play with regularly, join a backgammon club, and play in some tournaments.

11-7. The following will further improve your play in clubs and tournaments:
- *Obtain as much experience as possible*
- *Be in good mental and physical condition*
- *Become familiar with the specific rules*
- *Get to know your opponents*
- *Be a good sportsman*

As in all games and sports, practice makes perfect. Although you have learned the correct strategy, it will take a lot of experience to become a strong player. To perform well in a tournament, you will have to play well for several hours. Be in good mental and physical condition (and stay sober) so you can sustain a high caliber of play for several hours at a time.

Some of the rules, particularly for doubling, roll-over, and number of points needed to win a set or match, will vary from club to club and from tournament to tournament. You need to become familiar with the rules that your club or tournament uses.

If you join a club, you will become familiar with how the other club members play. Knowing how well your opponent plays, what type of game he plays, and what he does in certain situations will help you adjust your play to increase your chance of winning the match. For example, if your opponent likes to play back games, double him and play for a gammon to win a maximum number of points when he starts to position himself for a back game. Become familiar with your opponent's doubling strategy. If you enter a tournament where you aren't familiar with the other players, scout your potential opponents, if you can. If you finish a match early, go watch the match that will provide your next opponent.

Finally, always be a good sportsman. Be a gracious winner and a courteous loser so that you are a respected member of the club and participant in tournaments. Of course, winning a high percentage of your matches will also gain you much respect.

CONDUCTING TOURNAMENTS

A good way to become acquainted with and play other backgammon players is to join a local club. If there is no club in your area, perhaps you can organize one. You can also conduct occasional informal mini-tournaments. If there aren't enough players, then introduce this book to some of your friends and teach them how to play. There is a good chance that they will become as avid and good as you are.

Clubs usually conduct periodic tournaments and may compete against other clubs in regional tournaments. If your club needs help in organizing and conducting tournaments, use the following steps.

1. Determine and announce when and where the tournament will be conducted.

2. Establish and circulate the rules and conditions. The official rules provided in Appendix A (except Rules 20a and 21) should be used as the basic rules of play.

3. Decide the prizes, monetary or other, and collect an entry fee to pay for prizes and expenses.

4. Establish whether the tournament will consist of elimination matches or round-robin matches, and whether it will have a consolation bracket.

5. Set up the bracket if elimination matches are used. Seed the players or have them draw numbers to determine the player lineup in the bracket or round-robin.

An elimination match bracket is set up as shown in Figure 11-2. The winner of the match between Player 1 and Player 2 plays the winner of the match between Player 3 and Player 4, etc. If there are an uneven number of players, then one or more players get a first round bye. For example, if there are six players, there is no Seed 7 (Player 7) or Seed 8 (Player 2) so Seed 1 (Player 1) and Seed 2 (Player 8) get a bye (automatically win the first round and move to the second round). If there are only four players, there is no Seed 5 through 8 and the players start at the second round in Figure 11-2.

Figure 11-2

If the skill level is known for most or all of the players, the players should be seeded as shown in Figure 11-2. The best player is Seed 1, the next best is Seed 2, and so on. As you can see from Figure 11-2, this prevents the best players from playing each other in the first couple of rounds so they don't knock each other out of the tournament in the early rounds. This makes it possible (even likely) for the two best players to meet in the final round to determine the champion.

If there are 9 to 16 players, double the size of the bracket and add another round to determine the champion. Player 16 is Seed 2, etc. If there are 17 to 32 players, you double it again and add another round.

Each round should be a three-set match; that is, the player that wins two sets wins the match and round. The last (championship) round should be a five-set match. It can even be a seven-set match like baseball, basketball, and ice hockey championships, if time permits. Depending on the number of players (rounds) and time available, the number of sets in each match can be more or may have to be less. To keep the tournament timespan reasonable, the first round may have to be limited to a one-set match. If there is a large amount of time available, the number of sets in each match should be increased, rather than the number of points in each set, in order to further reduce the element of luck and impact of an unfortunate game. This also brings the doubling strategy near the end of a set into play more often. Seven-point sets should always be used.

With six to seven games in a seven-point set and an average game taking seven to eight minutes to play, a typical set requires around 48 minutes (6.1×7.9). So, an average three-set match will require about two hours or around 120 minutes (48×2.5) to play. Therefore, an eight-player (three-round) tournament consisting of three-set matches can usually be completed in six hours (3×2 hours). A 16-player tournament will take around eight hours.

Have a consolation bracket for the players that lose in the first two rounds of the main bracket. This ensures each player of being able to play at least two matches in the tournament. The elimination bracket is set up in a manner similar to the main bracket.

In a round-robin tournament, each player plays a match with every other player. If time doesn't permit a complete round-robin, each player plays as many other players as possible. If there are a lot of players, each match should be limited to one set so that each player can play as many other players as possible. The player that wins the most matches wins the tournament. If there is a tie, the champion is the player that beat the other tied player(s). If two or more players are still tied, a small elimination bracket for the players that are tied should be used to determine the champion. If there are only three players available for a mini-tournament, either a round-robin or a chouette should be played, as described in the next chapter.

Prizes should be awarded to the tournament champion, runner-up, and winner of the consolation bracket. The champion's prize should be considerably more valuable than the others.

If there is a large range of player skill levels, consider including a handicap to keep the matches and tournament challenging for the better players and give the less experienced players a more equitable chance of winning. The best way to include a handicap is to have the less experienced players start each set with one or more points. Handicaps are most appropriate for informal tournaments and casual play.

Backgammon is most enjoyable for everyone when it is played at a steady rapid pace. If slow play could be a problem in a tournament or casual play, a time limit penalty of one point should be set for each player in each set, like in some other games and most sports. Each player's playing time limit should be high enough (around 40 minutes) so that a reasonably rapid player will rarely reach it. After a player exceeds his time limit, his opponenrt should receive an additional point for each additional five minutes of playing time used during the set.

INTERNATIONAL TOURNAMENTS

Many international backgammon tournaments are conducted periodically. They are distinguished and festive events where the world's best players compete and the prize money is usually well over $100,000. The most prominent international tournaments are the World Championship and the World Cup. The World Championship is conducted annually, currently in Monte Carlo. The World Cup is held every two years in a United States city. The U.S. Open is a national tournament that is conducted every two years and has three divisions for different ability levels. There are many other international and national tournaments that are run periodically. There are also many state, regional, and city backgammon tournaments with much distinction and prize money.

In 1964, an annual international tournament was started in the Bahamas. Oswald Jacoby, who is also a world-class bridge player, won it from 1966 to 1968, and was the runner-up in 1969. There were 64 participants in this tournament each year. For a person to perform that well, skill has to be the dominant factor. If luck were a big factor, it would be unlikely for a person to win this tournament more than once. A dark horse rarely wins a tournament and the best players usually meet in the final round. There are a fairly small number of players in the world that repeatedly make it to the final rounds of the major tournaments.

12. VARIANTS

The backgammon variants are described in this chapter. Become familiar with them because some players may suggest that one or more of the variants be used. The roll-over is a variant and it is the only variant that should be used. Strongly encourage the use of the roll-over, but be reluctant to use any other variant. The use of any variant must be agreed upon by all players prior to starting to play.

Rules 20a and 21 for automatic doubles and alternate scoring methods (see Appendix A) are optional rules rather than variants. Most players and tournaments don't use them.

CHOUETTE

In a chouette, one person plays against two or more people. A chouette can be interesting and sociable. If there are four or more players, however, a mini-tournament should be conducted in which the players are paired up to play one against one in each round instead of playing a chouette. If there are three players, it's better to find a fourth player and have a mini-tournament than to play a chouette. However, if you only have three players, playing a chouette is preferable to sending a person away or having him kibitz.

If a chouette is appropriate, one person, who is in the box, plays against the other two. One person of the two-player team is the captain. The players of the two-player team jointly decide their moves and roll-over usage. If they cannot agree, the captain makes the decision. Each player of the two-player team can decide to double or accept a double individually, so two doubling cubes are needed.

The best way to play a chouette is to play a three-set match where the players rotate each set. Each player is the individual player (in the box), the captain, and the teammate for one set. Each player of the two-player team receives the points that they win in the set. The player that wins the most points in the three sets is the winner of the match.

OPENING ROLL

In this variant, the opening roll, where each player rolls one of his dice, merely determines which player wins the first turn. The player that wins the opening roll then rolls both of his dice to make his first move. In some uses of this variant, the player that wins the first turn can choose to play that roll or roll both of his dice. This allows the possibility of doubles for the first move of games, and gives the player that wins the first turn an added advantage. This variant isn't recommended because it makes luck a larger factor.

NO BACKGAMMONS

Some players think that winning a backgammon is the result of extraordinary luck so they do not allow backgammons. However, a backgammon is usually the result of considerable skill by the winner or an all-out back game that fails. Backgammons should always be allowed because they are an important part of the game.

JACOBY RULE (THE GAMMON CUBE)

In the Jacoby Rule (or gammon cube) variant, a gammon doesn't count unless at least one double has been accepted. The reasoning for this variant is that it will prevent uninteresting games from continuing when a player has a huge lead. It encourages a player with a huge lead to double his opponent out rather than trying to win a gammon. Actually, this objective isn't achieved often because a player should double as soon as he gains a substantial lead, before he has a huge lead. The only time this variant would come into play is in a game when a substantial lead becomes a huge lead in one round with no previous doubles, which doesn't happen often.
The problems with this variant are:
• It eliminates some of the strategy in deciding whether to double or continue to possibly win a gammon.
• It encourages players to take wild chances before the first double in each game since only one point can be lost.

THE BEAVER

In this variant the player that is doubled can accept, redouble, and retain possession of the cube, if he does so before the doubling player rolls. The beaver doesn't make sense for players who know the proper doubling strategy because a player should normally have more than a 70% chance of winning the game to double. The doubled player would be crazy to redouble with less than a 30% chance of winning the game.

ACEY-DEUCEY

In acey-deucey, the game starts with all men off the board. You start the game by entering men into your opponent's inner board as if they are on the bar. Once a man is entered, it can continue to be moved even though all of the men aren't yet entered. This makes the game more of a race than a strategy game. The 2-1 roll is magical in the game. Each time it's rolled, the player plays the 2-1, plays the doubles of his choice, and rolls again. This completely distorts the game each time a 2-1 is rolled and increases the element of luck.

SETTLEMENTS

Occasionally you may encounter a player who offers to end a game by giving the player that is in the lead a suggested number of points or amount of money. If you're willing to participate in the settlement, you then negotiate and agree upon the amount that the leader wins by ending the game. Never agree to use settlements because they aren't consistent with playing sets and matches.

APPENDIX A.
RULES OF THE GAME

The following are the official rules of backgammon (Rules 1 through 21). They have been accepted by the Card and Backgammon Committee of the Racquet and Tennis Club of New York, the International Backgammon Association, the Inter-Club League of New York, and essentially the rest of the world. The most recent significant revision to the rules occurred in 1931.

THE GAME

1. The game of backgammon is played by two persons.
2. 30 men, 15 of one color and 15 of another, are used, and are set up as shown in Figure 2-1 on a standard board of four quarters (boards) having six points each.
3. For entering and bearing off, the points in both inner boards are considered as numbered from 1 to 6, beginning with the point nearest the edge of the board.
4. Direction of play is from opponent's inner board to opponent's outer board, to player's outer board, and then to player's inner (home) board.
5. Play of the men is governed by two dice, rolled from a cup in which the dice are shaken before rolled.
6. Choice of seats, men, set-up, and dice shall be made by the player winning the opening roll.

THE ROLLS

7. For the opening roll, each player rolls a single die. Every tie requires another opening roll. Whoever rolls the higher number wins, and for his first move plays the numbers on both dice. After that, each player in turn rolls two dice.
8. The dice must be rolled together and come to rest flat (not cocked) on the board at the player's right; otherwise they must be rolled again.
9. If a roll is made before an opponent's play is completed, or if either

player touches a die before it has come to rest, the opponent of the offender may require a reroll.

10. A player must leave his dice on the board until his play is completed. Should he pick them up or turn them over before the completion of his play, the opponent may declare the play void and require the offender to replace the man or men moved and to roll again.

THE PLAY

11. The play of the men consists of:

a. Moving a man the exact number of points indicated by the number on a die rolled.

b. Entering a man, in the opponent's inner board, on a point corresponding to the number on a die rolled.

c. Bearing off a man in player's inner board—when no man is left outside that board or on the bar—from a point corresponding to the number on a die rolled, or as provided in Rule 15.

d. Doubles require four plays—if possible—of the die number rolled.

12. No play may be made that lands on a point held by two or more of the opponent's men.

13. When a play lands on a single man (blot) of the opponent, such man is "hit" and must be lifted and placed on the bar for entry in the player's inner board.

14. A player having a man on the bar may not play until that man has been entered.

15. Plays must be made for both dice if possible. Either number may be played first. If only one number can be played, and there is a choice, the higher must be played. In bearing off, a man may at all times be correctly borne off from the highest occupied point that is lower than the number indicated by the die. If a number is rolled for an unoccupied point, no man below can be borne off, for such number, while any man remains on a higher point.

16. Whenever a man has been moved correctly and quitted (the player's hand removed), that play cannot be changed.

ERRORS

17. If an error has been made in the set-up, either player may correct it prior to the completion of his first play.

18. If an error in play has been made, either player may require its correction before a subsequent roll, but not thereafter. The man played in error must be correctly played if possible.

SCORING

19. A game is won by the player who first bears off all of his men. A gammon (double game) is won if the opponent has not borne off a single man. This doubles the game value. A backgammon (triple game) is won if the opponent has not borne off a single man, and has one or more men in the winner's inner board or on the bar. This triples the game value.

20. The game value is raised:

a. **Automatically** By agreement, each tie of the opening roll may either double the previous game value or add one point to the previous value. Unless an understanding has been reached as to the method and limitation of automatic raises, they are not played.

b. **Voluntarily** Either player may offer the first double of the game value. After that, the right to double the previous value alternates, being always with the player who has accepted the last double. A double may be offered only when it is the player's turn to play and before he has rolled the dice. A double must be accepted or declined. The refusal of the double terminates the game, and the doubling player wins the game value at that time. Gammons and backgammons double or triple the last value.

21. By agreement, other methods of scoring may be used, such as the point game. In this, one point is scored by the winner for each man left in the opponent's inner board, two points are scored for each man left in the opponent's outer board, three points for each man left in the winner's outer board, and four points for each man left in the winner's inner board or on the bar.

Rules 20a and 21 apply only if both players agree to use them. Most players today modify Rule 16 such that a player signifies that his move is completed by picking up his dice; then the play cannot be changed if it is correct (legal). The move can be changed prior to picking up the dice.

THE CRAWFORD RULE

When a player gets to one point short of winning a set, the doubling cube cannot be used in the next game, but can be used again thereafter. See page 18 for more on this rule.

ROLL-OVER

See page 18 and Chapter 5.

SETS AND MATCHES

A player wins one point (initial basic game value) by winning a game if there are no doubles, gammon, or backgammon. A set should consist of seven points; the player that wins seven points first wins the set. By agreement, a set can consist of more or fewer points. The player that wins one or more sets wins the match. The number of sets that must be won to win the match must be established prior to starting a match.

APPENDIX B.
STRATEGY PRINCIPLES

All of the strategy principles are collected in this appendix for quick reference. While all of the strategy principles and sub-principles are important, the key principles are indicated by an asterisk. Since you probably cannot learn and remember all of the strategy instantly, learn the key principles first and then expand to the others. If you cannot remember all of the numbers, at least have a good feel for the chance of rolling specific numbers, hitting, making points, entering, bearing off, and winning the game for the various situations.

BASIC STRATEGY

BASIC GAME SAVVY

3-1. Have a comfortable playing environment so you can concentrate on the game
3-2.* Be able to play at a rapid pace, but do not rush
3-3. Become equally comfortable playing with either color men and with your inner board to your left or right
3-4. Insist on not using any of the variants or optional rules except the roll-over
3-5. Always check that opponent's move is legal; if opponent makes an illegal move that is unfavorable for you, have him correct it
3-6. Do not let your opponent know he made a mistake; that is, do not help him adjust or improve his game
3-7. Play to minimize impact of bad luck and take maximum advantage of good luck
3-8.* Never give up, even if it appears that you are hopelessly behind

PRIME STRATEGIC OBJECTIVE

3-9.* A blocking game is substantially better than a running game, about 65%
3-10.* Your prime strategy is to build a strong blockade as quickly as possible to trap one of the opponent's men; you will usually have nearly 26 rolls, if nec-

essary, to do this before he finishes bearing off (assuming you are not doubled out)

3-11. Only a slight advantage in winning games is needed to have a large advantage in winning matches

FUNDAMENTAL STRATEGY FOR WINNING

3-12. Priority for making points: your 5-, 7-, 4-, 3-, and 9-points, in that order

3-13.* You have a greater than 95% chance of winning a game when you trap one or more men behind a prime

3-14.* Move to form a six-point side prime, then caterpillar it into a true prime

3-15. When caterpillaring a prime, move your other men to the prime one at a time to optimize your chance of caterpillaring it

3-16. When caterpillaring a prime, put a blot in front of prime when necessary if there is little chance it will be trapped after entering if it is hit

3-17.* Achieve as even a distribution as possible

3-18. When considerably behind in a game or set, play more aggressively than usual

ROLLS REQUIRED TO START AND FINISH BEARING OFF

3-19.* Average roll is 8 pips

3-20.* Number of rolls required to reach inner board is shown in Figure 3-5

3-21. If no men are hit or trapped, it usually takes 11.5 rolls to get all men into your inner board

3-22. A running player requires around 21 rolls to win if not hit; around 26 rolls if you hit your opponent twice

HITTING PROBABILITY

3-23.* Chance of hitting a blot is shown in Table 3-2

3-24. Subtract one roll for each intermediate point covered when determining chance of hitting a blot

3-25. Subtract four rolls after adding chances of two men hitting

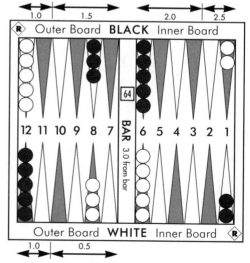

Figure 3-5

116

3-26. When leaving a shot, try to leave it so it can only be hit by a roll that is good to use elsewhere

3-27. Take risks early before opponent fills his inner board or has strong blockade

DOUBLING STRATEGY

PRIMARY DOUBLING PRINCIPLES

4-1.* Consider doubling with a greater than 62% chance of winning the game

4-2.* Accept double with a greater than 25% chance of winning the game

4-3. Early in a game, accept double with less than a 25% chance of winning game (around 22%) since you only need to achieve a 76% chance of winning in one of four games to win one of four games

4-4.* Optimum time to double occurs when you have the highest chance of winning the game and your opponent will still accept

4-5.* Doubling range as function of opponent's acceptance point is shown in Table 4-2

DOUBLING SITUATIONS

4-6. Consider doubling if two or more rolls ahead with one or more opponent men trapped behind blockade of four or more points

4-7.* Chance of winning game is shown in Table 4-3

4-8.* In straight race, consider doubling when greater than 5% ahead in pips with distribution equal to opponent; accept double if less than (5% + 3) pips behind

4-9.* Double when opponent is trapped behind your prime unless you have

Table 3-2

Points away	Rolls that hit	Chance of hitting
1	11	31%
2	12	33%
3	14	39%
4	15	42%
5	15	42%
6	17	47%
7	6	17%
8	6	17%
9	5	14%
10	3	8%
11	2	6%
12	3	8%
16	1	3%
20	1	3%
24	1	3%

Table 4-2

Opponent acceptance pt.	Doubling range
30%	65%-75%
25%	70%-80%
20%	75%-85%

Table 4-3

Rolls ahead	Blockade points	Men trapped	Chance of winning
2	4	1	63%
2	4	2	70%
2	5	1	70%
2	5	2	75%
3	<4	0	70%
3	4	1	73%
3	4	2	75%
3	5	1	75%
3	5	2	80%

good chance for gammon

4-10. Double when you get 3 rolls ahead unless you have a man trapped, opponent has a strong blockade, or you have more than one blot in danger; it takes only a 2-roll lead if it is likely that you will become uninterlocked without getting hit

OTHER DOUBLING CONSIDERATIONS

4-11. Usually double if opponent has a large flaw in his position

4-12.* Do not double when you have a reasonable (more than 50%) chance of winning gammon

4-13. To gammon opponent, you usually have to trap three or more men behind a prime; then chance is around 60% for gammon

4-14. Usually resign when more than 3 rolls behind

4-15. Double earlier than usual when playing a less experienced player

4-16. Often one player can double by his seventh roll

4-17. With two good players, the cube does not reach 8 often; most games it is 1 or 2; some games it becomes 4

ROLL-OVER STRATEGY

BASIC ROLL-OVER STRATEGY

5-1. Do not let frustration or emotions determine when you use your roll-over

5-2.* Use roll-over when:

• *Opponent gets a 1-in-18 (or 1-in-36) roll that really hurts*

• *Opponent gets a roll that will allow him to double you out*

• *Your roll allows opponent to double you out*

• *You have more than a 70% chance of putting opponent in deep hole and miss it*

• *Opponent rolls double 4s, 5s, or 6s in a straight race*

• *You do not bear at least two men off with just a couple rolls left in game*

• *Opponent bears off more than two men with just a couple rolls left in game*

5-3. If you have your roll-over, you can take a risk to put your opponent in a deep hole

OTHER ROLL-OVER CONSIDERATIONS

5-4. In over 80% of games a player is doubled out, so less than 20% of games are won by completely bearing off

5-5. In more than 60% of games the players are still interlocked when one of them is doubled out

5-6. In only around 15% of games do the players become uninterlocked without a double

5-7.* Consider the roll-over in conjunction with doubling strategy

5-8.* Roll-over is worth approximately 4% game or approximately 7% pips in a straight race

OPENING AND EARLY-GAME MOVES

OPENING MOVES

6-1.* Best opening moves:
- 1-1: make 5-point and 7-point
- 2-2: make 4-point and 11-point
- 3-3: make 5-point and 3-point
- 4-4: make 5-point
- 5-5: make 3-point
- 6-6: make both 7-points
- 3-1: make 5-point
- 6-1: make 7-point
- 4-2: make 4-point
- 6-5, 6-4, and 6-3: move runner
- 5-3: move two men to outer board; if opponent has split runners, make 3-point
- 6-2: move runner with 6 and man to 11-point with 2
- 2-1, 4-1, and 5-1: move man to outer board and use 1 to split runners
- 3-2, 4-3, 5-2, and 5-4: move two men to outer board

EARLY-GAME MOVES AND STRATEGY

6-2.* Generally better to make your 5-point than to hit; otherwise, hit

6-3.* Be reluctant to leave a blot in your inner board

6-4. When determining best move, compare "net positive" of each alternative where "net positive" is number of rolls that will make an important point next move minus number of opponent's rolls that will hit you

6-5.* Split runners with a 1 or 2 roll if there is no other beneficial way of using it

6-6.* Do not make your 1-point or 2-point too early. This puts men out of play, makes it difficult to build a side prime, and wastes pips in being able to start bearing off

6-7. If you roll 6-6 early, your priority should shift toward a running game

6-8. If your opponent has blots on your 1-point and 3-points and you roll 5-5 early in a game, play a wipeout game by making your 1-point and 3-point, hitting both blots

MID-GAME STRATEGY

MID-GAME MOVE STRATEGY

7-1.* You should hit an opponent's blot, make a point for your blockade or elsewhere, bring builder(s) into position to make a point, or move a runner, in that order of priority

7-2. By fifth roll start giving priority to escaping with runners

7-3.* Be reluctant to give up 12-point too soon; try to escape with runners first

7-4. Do not give up your 6-point or 8-point until you are ready to start bearing off

7-5. Usually do not hit a blot in your inner board unless you can point on it

7-6. If you can hit two blots, you should usually do so unless they are in your inner board

7-7. The "hit and run" can be an effective move

7-8. Usually enter a man from bar onto lowest possible point

7-9. In at least 70% of games, you will hit at least two of opponent's men

7-10. Blockade with forward gap is better than solid blockade if opponent's man is next to it

7-11.* When both you and opponent are trapped behind a blockade, timing is critical because the player that has to collapse his blockade first will probably lose

7-12.* When behind in game, give some priority to making opponent's 4-, 5-, or 7-point

7-13.* When more than 1 roll behind, stay back to hit rather than run

7-14. Leave an indirect shot, if necessary, to avoid leaving a direct shot later

7-15. You can be more willing to leave a shot when opponent has blot(s) in his inner board or does not have a blockade

7-16. If you have to leave a direct shot, hit an opponent's man if possible

7-17. If you have to leave a blot, try to leave it on an important point to make

7-18. If you have to leave two shots, try to leave them so it takes the same number to hit them

7-19.* Take a chance to win a gammon or backgammon if it doesn't greatly reduce chance of winning game

PROBABILITIES

7-20.* Chance of entering one man from bar is shown in Table 7-1

7-21. Chance of entering two men from bar with one roll is shown in

Table 7-1

Number of points covered	Rolls that enter	Chance of entering one man
1	35	97%
2	32	89%
3	27	75%
4	20	56%
5	11	31%

Table 7-2

7-22.* Chance of making a point is shown in Table 7-3

7-23.* Chance of rolling a specific number is shown in Table 7-4

7-24.* Chance of rolling a 5 or 6 is shown in Table 7-5

7-25.* Chance of rolling a specific combination such as 6-1 is shown in Table 7-6

Table 7-2

Number of points covered	Rolls that enter	Chance of entering two men
1	25	69%
2	16	44%
3	9	25%
4	4	11%
5	1	3%

Table 7-3

Number of builders	Chance of making point
2	7%
3	19%
4	39%
5	61%
6	92%

Table 7-4

Number of rolls	Chance of rolling number
1	31%
2	52%
3	67%

Table 7-5

Number of rolls	Chance of 5 or 6
1	56%
2	80%
3	91%

Table 7-6

Number of rolls	Chance of combo
1	6%
2	11%
3	16%

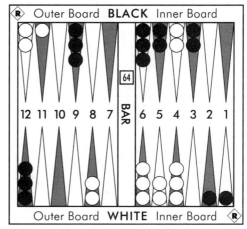

Figure 7-15

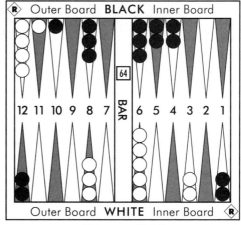

Figure 7-16

MID-GAME DOUBLING STRATEGY

7-26. In Figures 7-15 and 7-16, white has 66% chance of winning and can consider doubling

7-27. In Figures 7-17 and 7-18, white has 70% chance of winning and should double; black should accept

7-28. In Figure 7-19 white has 74% chance of winning and should double; black should accept

7-29. In Figure 7-20 white has 76% chance of winning and should double; black should resign

7-30. In Figure 7-21 white has 83% chance of winning and should wait to double

<u>END-GAME STRATEGY</u>

END-GAME MOVE STRATEGY

8-1.* Timing can be critical when both players have to break an outer board point to bring the men to safety

8-2.* When you are nearly uninterlocked and ahead, carefully try to turn the game into a straight race

8-3. When you are one or more rolls behind, hit a man even if you have to leave a shot

8-4. In a straight race, get all of your men to your outer board before you move more men to your inner board

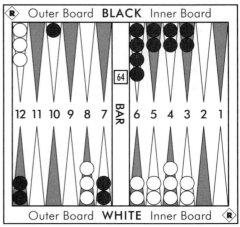

Figure 7-17

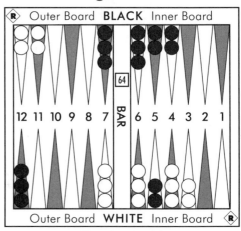

Figure 7-18

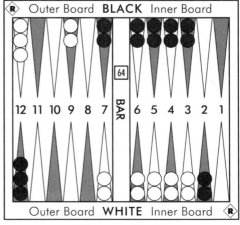

Figure 7-19

122

8-5.* In a straight race, get all your men into your inner board as quickly as possible, even if it means stacking men on your 6-point

END-GAME DOUBLING STRATEGY

8-6. Pip count is about 54 when all men are in inner board evenly distributed

8-7.* Pip count is usually about 65 when last man enters inner board because high points are heavily loaded

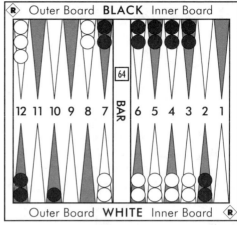

Figure 7-20

BEARING OFF

BEARING OFF WHEN INTERLOCKED

9-1.* When bearing off with opponent in your inner board or on bar, vacate the highest point first rather than creating open points between your men

9-2.* When bearing off with opponent in your inner board or

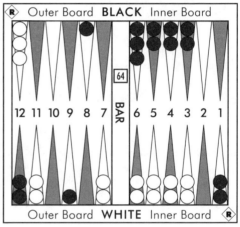

Figure 7-21

on bar, avoid leaving odd number of men on highest two points. Avoid leaving three men on highest point if it is less than 6-point

9-3. When bearing off with opponent in your inner board or on bar, remember that you are not required to bear a man off if there is an alternate legal move

9-4. Remember that you can play the dice in either order

BEARING OFF WHEN NOT INTERLOCKED

9-5. When bearing off and not interlocked, always bear a man off in preference to moving a man within the inner board

9-6.* For bearing off, add ¹/₄ roll for each extra empty low point and each extra man on high points

9-7.* When there are only a few rolls left in the game, double if your opponent needs at least as many rolls as you to bear off

9-8. Double with more than a 50% chance of winning when only one roll is left in game

9-9.* Chance of bearing one or two men off with one roll is shown in Table 9-1

9-10. Chance of bearing two men off in two rolls is shown in Table 9-2

9-11. When bearing off, leave one man on a high point rather than two on lower points

9-12. When you have to bear the rest of your men off next turn, maximize your chance of doing so

Table 9-1

Points man/men are on	Rolls that bear off	Chance of bearing both off
6 & 4	8	22%
6 & 3	10	28%
6 & 1	15	42%
4 & 3	17	47%
5 & 2	19	53%
3 & 2	25	69%
2 & 2	26	72%
6	27	75%
4 & 1	29	81%
5	31	86%
4	34	94%

THE BACK GAME

BACK GAME DOUBLING STRATEGY

10-1.* Double opponent back game if chance of winning gammon is not good (less than 40%)

10-2.* Decline double when in back game

CONDUCTING A BACK GAME

Table 9-2

Points men are on	Chance of bearing both off
6 & 6	78%
6 & 5	88%
6 & 4	93%
6 & 3	97%

10-3.* The 1-point and 3-point are best for back game; next best are 2-point and 3-point

10-4. When playing a back game, try to time it so that you have a full inner board when you hit opponent

10-5. To obtain the proper timing in a back game, you may have to leave blots to entice your opponent to hit them to slow you down

10-6.* In a back game don't wait too long to start running with your back men

10-7. When you must hit a man, maximize your chance of hitting even if you have to leave a shot

PLAYING AGAINST A BACK GAME

10-8. When playing against a back game top priority is to move safely

10-9.* When playing against a back game move so a 5 or 6 can be safely played on next roll

MATCH AND TOURNAMENT STRATEGY

SET AND MATCH STRATEGY

11-1. When you lose a game, minimize your loss to one or two points by using correct doubling strategy, avoiding a gammon, and rarely (if ever) losing a backgammon

Table 11-1

Points from set			
You	Opp.	Double	Accept
1	2	Do not double	>50% game
1	3	Do not double	>40% game
2	1	Immediately	N/A
2	2	>55% game	>25% game
2	3	>75% game	>30% game
2	4	>75% game	>30% game
3	1	>55% game	N/A
3	2	>65% game	>25% game
4	1	>55% game	N/A
4	2	>60% game	>20% game

11-2.* When near end of set, use doubling strategy shown in Table 11-1

11-3.* When you are ahead in a set, you need a larger chance of winning than normal to double or accept a double; when you are behind in a set, double and accept a double with a smaller chance of winning than normal

11-4. Be more reluctant than normal to do something if it could take your opponent to the Crawford Rule game

11-5. When opponent will win set if he wins game, go all out to win game even at risk of being gammoned or backgammoned

11-6. On average, six to seven games are played in a seven-point set

TOURNAMENT STRATEGY

11-7. The following will further improve your play in clubs and tournaments:
• Obtain as much experience as possible
• Be in good mental and physical condition
• Become familiar with the specific rules
• Get to know your opponents
• Be a good sportsman

INDEX